300 Days, 300 Nights

A Historical Chronicle of Drill Music's Emergence and the Tragedies it Brought

by

ACE BOOGIE

300 Days, 300 Nights

Copyright © 2024 Ace Boogie all rights reserved.

No part of this book may be reproduced, distributed or transmitted in any form by any means, graphics, electronics, or mechanical, including photocopy, recording, taping, or by any information storage or retrieval system, without permission in writing from the publisher, except in the case of reprints in the context of reviews, quotes, or references.

Printed in the United States of America.

ISBN: 978-1-7366158-7-4

Table of Contents

Disclaimer --- 5
Artist notes --- 6
Introduction --- 7
Chapter One --- 10
Chapter Two --- 19
Chapter Three --- 29
Chapter Four -- 60
Chapter Five -- 81
Chapter Six --- 91
Chapter Seven -- 102
Chapter Eight -- 110
Chapter Nine --- 122
Chapter Ten -- 143
Chapter Eleven --- 154
Chapter Twelve --- 161
Chapter Thirteen --- 171
Chapter Fourteen --- 182
Chapter Fifteen -- 189
Chapter Sixteen -- 200
Conclusion --- 207
References --- 210

Disclaimer

The information presented in this book is based on research, interviews, and available sources. While every effort has been made to ensure the accuracy of the information provided, the author and publisher cannot guarantee the completeness or timeliness of the details presented. Readers are encouraged to conduct their own research and verify the facts presented in this book. The author and publisher shall not be held responsible for any errors, omissions, or inaccuracies in the content, nor for any consequences that may arise from the use of this information."

Artist notes

This book was written from the perspective of a journalist with a commitment to fairness and accuracy and as a street dude. In my quest to uncover the truth, I delved deep into the research surrounding this topic to present a comprehensive and insightful narrative. It is essential to note that the book was crafted to resonate with a diverse audience, catering to multiple genders and various walks of life. My intention was not to alienate or offend any reader but rather to shed light on the complexities and nuances of the subject matter.

Introduction

Rap Music and the streets have always had a close connection, one that seems to have grown even closer with the emergence of Drill Music. The Chicago music scene illustrates the lifestyle of low-income residents whose lives have been plagued with violence and poverty. Chief Keef, Lil Durk, and King Von, some of the celebrities of drill music, rose from poverty but could not escape the violent lifestyle they knew all too well.

In 2011, on the Southside of Chicago, a 16-year-old young man spent 60 days on house arrest for a shooting in his neighborhood. While it might sound implausible that a teenager was on house arrest for charges related to firearms, this was one of the lighter cases that year because others were not as lucky. Between the years 2011 and 2014, more than 19 people were killed in the same Chicago vicinity. They were all victims of Drill music and rival gang members who died in a series of back-to-back retaliatory street wars. Such was the relationship between Drill music and the street.

From house arrest while in the custody of his grandmother, the restless Keith Farrelle Cozart, who adopted the alias "Chief Keef," jump-started his career with a single titled "I Don't Like." This single essentially brought the Drill genre to the limelight.

On the street, "Drill" has several meanings. It can mean "to shoot someone," "to fight," or "retaliate." Drill music is similar to rap, but was inspired by Trap music, focusing on gun violence, street battles, and poverty that artists like Chief Keef and others faced in their neighborhoods. Drill lyrics are often intense, raw, and loaded with profanity, unlike the play on words and structure you find in rap. The artists are mostly harsh, and straightforward, attacking one another with their lyrics. For the large part, these songs express the brutality of gun violence and the unending gang wars on the streets.

Drill music stands out and distances itself from rap and trap by emphasizing crime, violence, and death in the way it is presented to the listener. Some people can't comprehend that Drill music keeps calling you when all you know is the streets. And to some, it's like a bitch with good head; when she calls, you must respond.

Even when these artists have made millions, and moved out of the ghetto, the street lifestyle is not easy to walk away from. To sustain the money they have made, violence, retaliation, hate, drugs, and pain need to continue to seep from the beats into the ears of those who understand the lifestyle of Drill artists.

The drill genre is fast gaining popularity through online streaming platforms like Apple Music, Soundcloud, Spotify, and YouTube. The internet allows artists to upload and share their music uncensored, thereby provoking intrigue for their fans. This easy means of distribution has paved the way for the rise in the popularity of Drill music across the globe. It's a genre of music that lends voice to millions of African Americans, and the people that relate to their plight.

To continue giving a voice to these millions of African American male and female listeners who face violence daily, Drill artists feel the need to stay connected to the streets. They have to remember they're the voice of the voiceless, that most of their fan base hear their war stories, and struggles within the artist's music.

What many professionals will tag as amateur video is the exact thing that captivates the viewers of Drill music videos because it's easy to relate to. The videos are a representation of who they are, their neighborhood, and the lifestyle they live. A typical Drill music video looks like a one-take shot with dreaded young boys and girls coming and going off-camera, wielding different shades of firearms, while marijuana and other drugs billowing in the air, altering the visibility of the viewers. The viewer can relate to these grimy-looking youngsters from the ghetto. They identify with their pains and see themselves in them.

Over the years, Drill music and its artists have faced stiff criticism and resistance for the lawlessness and brutal nature of the genre. Most of these artists have been known to be involved in violent crimes from their teen years through the rest of their careers. Many young men and women who had bright futures were gunned down suddenly, while many languished in various prisons. Drill rappers often end up falling victim to the same violence they showcase in their music. For instance, the recent murder of Pop Smoke, who was shot and killed in 2020, is just a reminder of the numerous young people whose blood has been shed on the street.

No one would have known today that we would be talking about these big-name artists as much as the murders committed around them. Names like Chief Keef, Lil Durk, and others will be explored in this book. Their stories turned out to be an urban novel and gangster movie in one. The main difference is that this is not entertainment; real lives were involved and lost. They were real actors; no do-overs. Once you got drilled, the game was over. The real nature of it was the main attraction for most ghettos across America.

From Black Disciples (BD) to Gangster Disciples (GD), it's a story with a lot of confusion and misunderstanding. It has a life of its own, so much so, that when diving in, you might come out more confused. It's a story with several layers, and we plan to explore and unravel them all. The best place to start is where and how it all began. Now, let's do a drill.

Chapter One

A Brief History and Impact of Drill Music Across the Globe

The emergence of Chief Keef in 2012 from the Chicago Drill movement looked like instant folklore. That is because Drill music has always been associated with violence and deadly gang rivalries. No one thought the hyper-real and hyper-sound would one day make Chicago the hip-hop Mecca. Even more mind-boggling is that Drill music has accelerated the rise of hip-hop in countries like Ireland, Australia, Ghana, and particularly in England.

The pure energy that characterized the original Drill movement of Chicago has since been exported to the streets of England, helping rappers speak their truth with plain honesty and create a shift away from the previously dominant Grime, which was the UK type of rap. Politicians have blamed the rise of Drill music for increasing gang violence in London. Many fear that the streets of London are fast becoming like its Chicago counterpart- soaked with the blood of teenagers who fell victim to gang rivalries. On the other hand, artists and activists are rising to the defense of Drill music and seeing it as a symptom of racism and economic oppression.

For all the jibes about UK pop being old and uninspiring, it is surprising that it's the energy from the UK Drill that influenced the emergence of Drill music in New York. Artists like Divio Foreign and Sheff G have been at the forefront leading the cadences and melodies of NYC drill owe much to the UK's rising stars. Notable hit Drill songs out of New York like "Welcome To The Party" by Pop Smoke and "Suburban 1& 2" by 22Gz were all products of London drill producers.

Drill music is a part of hip-hop history with its roots in Chicago. However, it has become a mainstream language of violence and struggles globally, hence the need to review its development and broad reach.

Chicago, The Home of Drill Music

No honest conversation about Drill music can occur without due respect to Chicago, where it all started. The Drill music that shocked the world in 2012 was made up of several components. Most notable was the undisguised violent lyrics and chaotic sounds that showed the realities of the artists' world.

With its foundation in the South Side inner-city of Chicago, Drill music turned out to be the voice of a generation reflecting the harsh realities of living in low socio-economic neighborhoods. The dominance of gang-related crimes and the rapid rise of violent deaths resulted in the term "Chiraq" being used to compare these neighborhoods with war-torn countries like Iraq. According to a 2016 report by the National Post, more than 135 people were shot dead in the first quarter of that year in the South Side of Chicago, more than in New York City and LA put together.

The Chicago Drill music scene, predominantly dominated by street gangs, was run by teens and young adults and existed long before the 16-year-old Keith Cozart aka, Chief Keef, dropped his first mixtapes, "The Glory Road," and "Bang" in 2011. The buzz has always been there. However, Chief Keef can be credited with the rise to the subgenre's mainstream when he combined with another teenager Tavaras Taylor to shoot a local music video. At the time, the former was still under house arrest.

The raw production and overly authentic lyrics represented the ordeal of the rap community, which similar communities across the globe identified with. The music video, shot in Keef's grandmother's room, was devoid of fanfare and decorations that characterized a professional set. It was just teenagers with tattoos all over their bodies, smoking and wielding firearms as they shook their dreads back and forth while jumping in and out of camera view. The scene caught the attention of the world.

In 2014, after a remix with Kanye West, Pusha T, 2 Chainz, and Big Sean, Chief Keef hit, and Noisey's "Chiraq" rose to the top 100. Keef rose to prominence and was known more after he worked with other big names like Lady Gaga. Following in this rise to global view was Lil Durk (who also featured in Keef's "I Don't Like" hit), Lil Reese, and the GBE influence. These names and others quickly rose to prominence and became a part of Drill's hip-hop history.

After the rise to the mainstream of "I Don't Like," some complex realities of the industry rocked Chief Keef's career. In 2013, he signed with Interscope and later that year released "Finally Rich" and his biggest commercial hits, "Love Sosa," and "Hate Being Sober."

Although "Finally Rich" received scathing reviews and debuted at number 29 on the Billboard 200, it has been certified as gold by the Recording Industry Association of America (RIAA). Following growing tension between Keef and Interscope, the latter dropped the artist in 2014. The departure from Interscope launched Keef into more adventurous years of musical classics. He dropped hits like "Macaroni Time," "Faneto," and "Earned It," among other singles and other projects.

Even with no major label signing ad marketing since his break-up with Interscope, Keef was able to stay true to his Drill origin and the creative styles and freedom that come with it.

The Chicago Drill Scene Today

Chief Keef and other artists kept the Drill music scene alive, especially during Keef's Interscope days. These artists include e the late Fredo Santana, Lil Reese, Ballout, and OTF's Lil Durk, and other artists not related to Keef, such as Lil Bibby, G Herbo, King L, and Montana of 300. These guys have earned the right to be called leaders in the subgenre because they have stayed true to the style of Drill music. Although, some have refined the style while others have improved the technical rap style.

Veterans like late FBG Duck and Rooga are still doing big numbers, while new entrants like King Von and Polo G are asserting themselves in the hip-hop mainstream. This mixture of the old and new leaders has kept the Chicago Drill on the radar on the streets and in the commercial game.

The bigger news is how the gospel of Drill music has spread beyond the streets of Chicago to faraway cities beyond the shores of the United States. Drill music has now sprung up in towns and places where most people least expect it.

The London Drill

Given the characteristics of the Drill style of rapping and what it represents, you will be forgiven if you conclude that the next big city most influenced by Chicago Drill was a neighboring mid-Western city like Detroit. However, it was not. It was not even an American city, neither was it a North American one. It was London. This always surprises many Americans because the average fan sees the United Kingdom as a royal and orthodox setup. Many did not foresee that a Black artist from London and the neighboring cities would play a massive role in the transition of Drill music.

The birth of London Drill followed the massive success of Chief Keef's "I Don't Like" in 2012-2013. Although London Drill music is devoid of the firearms that its Chicago counterpart was notorious for; the gang culture still looked similar, with the hood-by-hood structure but with less organized violence. Instead of guns, the gangs wield bladed weapons like Knightly swords and 15-inch hunting knives.

Groups like 150 and 67 from Brixton can be credited with pioneering Drill music in London. Other solo and group artists include Harlem, Spartans, and Tottenham-based OFB. They have pushed Drill music into the UK's mainstream.

Followers of London Drill music always refer to "Kennington Where It Started" by Harlem Spartans as the evolution of Drill from lively underground wave to UK rap.

The Distinctive Nature of UK Drill

Musically and culturally, the United Kingdom's Drill is different from the Chicago version. There are still similarities in violence amongst teenagers, young adults, and rival gangs, but the music differs in style. UK Drill gives more room for cold, sparse beats with, and sliding 808s, and carries more vocals. A good example and reference point are "Drillers and Trappers" by Headie One and RV and "Double Tap Diaries" by Digga D.

Vocally, UK Drill artists use more punchlines, metaphors, and double entendre within tight flows. Due to Drill's success on the UK charts, there has been more emphasis on melody. Artists like Russ and Headie One are adept solo melodizers. Most Drill artists reach out to the adjacent sing-rap kings of UK hip-hop for waiver hooks and verses, including D-Block Europe, M. Huncho, and Nafe Smallz.

London Drill keeps growing in structure across Europe, Canada, and even in the United States. Like in Chicago, UK Drill has focused the public's attention on the stark realities of the low-income youth of color in London. Also, as in American politics, where politicians like Rahm Emanuel blame drill culture for all the violence in Chicago, British politicians are pointing fingers at Drill music as the source of the unrest rather than as a symptom.

Major British publications such as The Guardian, BBC, and The Independent have written extensively about Drill music and the government's failure to address the issues that affect young Black Brits.

New York City Drill Music

Shockingly, Drill music is the first hip-hop cultural movement in which United Kingdom artists influenced an American trend, especially in New York City. The city has seen the re-emergence of its version of the Drill movement coming from across the Atlantic. It's like exporting the raw version of a product, then importing it back to the country of origin after refining it and turning it into a finished product.

Like the London Drill move, the pioneers of Drill music in New York were inspired by the Chicago Drill artists who clearly copied the real gang life block-by-block. It would be incorrect to conclude that London Drill birthed NYC drill; however, many NYC artists have taken their sonic cues, cadences, and production style from the London Drill artists. A good example is Pop Smoke's "Welcome To The Party." which was produced by East Londoner 808Melo, who has also worked with artists like K. Trap and Headie One.

Sharing similar lifestyles and sounds, several NYC Drill leaders are Afro-Caribbeans and Afro-Latino Americans like their London counterparts who were first-generation Black Brits. Some prominent examples include Sheff G, who has both Haitian and Trinidadian backgrounds, 22Gz, of Guyanese descent, and late Pop Smokes, a mixture of Jamaican and Panamanian. This shared cultural background explains the ties between the two worlds. London rappers and their fans were some of the earliest supporters of NYC Drill.

The majority of NYC drillers are from Brooklyn, and just as we have in London and Chicago, the NYC cliques and gangs are seeing their stories gain attention and validation through rap. Not much is known about the street setups of the gangs and their rivalries; however, through Drill music, the Woos and Chos groups have been identified.

The Distinctive Nature of the New York Drill

The unique voices and rhymes of the NYC Srill artists show the local street stories of these marginalized youths. Producers like CashMoneyAP and WondaGurl are creating the newer version of Drill sounds from Brooklyn and London, as seen in tracks like Pop Smoke's "Christopher Walking". The rise of NYC drill might push the subgenre over the top like it did to trap music, which became a vital part of the music industry. Today we see trap components in pop, rap, and country hits; the same might gradually happen with Drill music.

Drill artists' vocal presence characterizes New York. They are wordy, perform technically with rap, and leave room between the bars hoping to fill it with their voices. This is evident in Pop Smoke's "Shake the Room," "Foreigner," and Sheff G's "Feel Ah Way." They have the UK Drill structure, only not as cold and minimal. NYC Drill artists often prefer busier beats than their UK counterparts. UK Drillers enjoy the space to get off the wordplay and punchlines, while NY artists like to bellow short bars that linger as the beats rampage.

For clarity, compare two examples of bare-bones UK Drill production "Already" by Headie One and "Double Tap Days" by Digga, with beats and artistic choice, to the NYC ones like Pop Smoke's "Dior," and "Fivio Foreign's Wetty."

Drill Making the Rounds

These days, Drill music can be heard worldwide; ONEFOUR, influenced by UK Drill, has a strong base in Sidney. With international collaboration fast becoming a thing, the Sidney-based

Drill artist recently collaborated with ASAP Ferg on "Say It Again," which premiered on 6th May 2020 and has more than 3.6 million views. These cross-pollination collaborations were most notable when UK Drill legends Skengdo and AM's partnered with the Godfather of Drill, Chief Keef, in 2018 for "Pit Bulls."

The influence of Drill is also seen in prominent rap artists like Drake. He employed JB Made on his drill track "Demons," ft. Fivio Foreign and Sosa Greek. JB and these other artists are big players in the New York Drill scene. In a statement to Billboard.com, JB observed the benefits of artists like Drake getting involved in the Drill scene. "Drake jumping on Drill is one of the best things that could've happened for the genre. He's a huge artist who's tapping into a sound that has already blown up over here."

In the UK space, Drill artists like Headie One and RV lead the modern Drill sounds with the release of certified banger, "Like Usher" in 2020. These are attempts to dust off the negative stigma associated with Drill music. Drill music is on the rise globally and so are the critics of its repetitive violent lyrics and videos. For instance, YouTube removed Drill videos from its platform as of November 2018; more than 90 drill videos were taken down. Several mainstream artists have received injunctions on their performances which hinders them from going on Nationwide tours. In another example, AM and Skendo recently pleaded guilty to violating their injunctions.

Following the constant criticism, drill music is undergoing several modifications. For example, artists like DigDat and Poundz have incorporated dance moves into their acts which changes the perception of Drill and keeps giving it more airtime. Amid these modifications, two academics from University College London, Kleinberg, and McFarlane, wrote in an essay, "There is no publicly available empirical evidence that Drill music language incited violent crime."

Irrespective of the increased condemnation and criticism of the aggressive and frequent tragic lifestyles accompanying Drill music, it has continued to gain audiences and performers from across the globe. However, it is pertinent to find out why this particular subgenre is associated with so much bloodshed, violence, and criminal activities. Everywhere the Drill style of music goes, there's always concern about the violence that accompanies it. To understand how we got here, we have to go back to the origin of Drill' where it all started, the characters involved, and their contributions.

In essence, you cannot talk about drill music without talking about Chicago, where it originated from; similarly, the story of Chicago is incomplete without the street gangs and the various crimes and murders that surround the subgenre. To tell the story correctly, we must talk about two key individuals who played a vital role in shaping the history of Chicago street gangs-David Barksdale and Larry Hoover. The story of these men cannot be told separately because their worlds crossed paths several times, and they had to work together for a long time. As we said before, this is a story with many layers, and we plan to explore them.

It is a tale of gang rivalries, crime, advocacy, and death. This story has everything you cannot imagine in it.

Chapter Two

The History of King David Barksdale

He was born May 24, 1947, in Sallis, Mississippi, to Virginia and Charlie. David Barksdale was officially named Donise David Barksdale, and he was the seventh child out of thirteen. In 1957, his family moved to Chicago, Illinois. Within three years of his arrival in the city, Barksdale assumed the responsibilities of a notorious gang leader.

Meanwhile, Larry Hoover, the stuttering young dude from Mississippi, would later become one of the biggest names in gangster history, not just in America, but in the world. He ranks up there with the likes of Al Capone.

The story of the Black Disciples is intertwined with that of David Barksdale. It has its roots in the days of the civil rights movements and how they tackled the challenges that plagued their communities. From the impoverished and frustrated communities of Englewood to the rough parts of Hyde Park, gangs were springing up all over the place to speak and fight for their communities. At the same time, the Gangster and Disciples were formed by teenage boys from the neighborhood. They would later evolve into a fundamental force to be reckoned with as they grew in numbers and organization.

Back in 1958, the rich white greaser youths bullied several Black teenagers in the poor Northern half of Hyde Park and the impoverished Southern Kenwood areas of Englewood. Before it was deemed unconstitutional in the late 40s, Hyde Park had consistently enforced restrictive racial covenants. Later, Black American families started moving into the older, Northern section of Hyde Park and the surrounding areas. As the neighborhoods of Southern Kenwood became more affordable around the 50s, more Blacks moved into the area. Additionally, more Black families moved into Englewood, which the Italians previously dominated. This would later lead to bullying of the newly settled Black families. There were white and Black gangs from other neighborhoods outside Hyde Park, Englewood, and Kenwood that invaded and bullied these young people.

As the bullying and gang activities continued, young Black boys between 11 and 13 from Englewood, Kenwood, and Hyde Park came together, first as friends and later to create a club that would fight against a common enemy. While searching for a name for their group, they flipped through the bible, and the idea of using "Disciple" jumped at them. So, to sound intimidating to their enemies, they decided to go with the name "Devil's Disciple." Consequently, the Devil's Disciple was formed. They immediately set out to mark their territories, which started with a heavy presence at 53rd and Kimbark in Hyde Park, 49th and Dorchester in Kenwood, and between 56th Street and 67th Steet Englewood.

The Disciples initially operated with no central leadership and kept their activities away from the press. Some of their founding members included David Barksdale, Prince Old Timer, Mingo Shread, Kilroy, Leonard Longstreet, Night Walker, Richard "Champ" Strong, and others. The Disciples grew strong and had their headquarters at the Hyde Park interchange of 53rd and Kimbark. In 1958, the gang adopted the Star of David, pitchfork, and the devil's tail with horns as their symbols.

The Rebels, a white street gang made up of 2,000 young men, were the first main rivals of the Devil's Disciple. They had their bases in Gage Park, Englewood, and West Englewood. The Disciples also rivaled other Black gangs in Englewood like the Egyptian Cobras, who moved to the neighborhood from the West side of Chicago in 1958. Furthermore, the Disciples battled another street gang called the Blackstone Raiders, who settled along Garfield Boulevard. The

Blackstone Raiders later changed to Blackstone Rangers and finally Black P. Stones.

In 1959, the Devil's Disciple made their biggest territory acquisition as they settled into the Western part of the Woodlawn community, controlling more than 65% of the neighborhood. The other portion was under the control of Blackstone Rangers and the Egyptian Cobras who had settled there.

Between 1958 and 1961, there was a White flight from these areas as more black families moved in and created recruitment opportunities for the Devil's Disciple. By 1961, the Disciples were already the most feared and powerful gang in Englewood. On the other hand, the Italian greaser gangs were growing weaker by the day.

In 1961, at just 14 years old, David Barksdale took over the reins of the Devil's Disciple. He was directly in control of the Englewood branch of the Disciples territory. He appointed Mingo as the leader over Hyde Park and Kenwood in what would later be known as the "East Side Disciples." Barksdale quickly settled down and started absorbing several small gangs in the South Side. The catch for all the absorbed groups was that they could all keep their names if they wanted to, but the last name must be "Disciple." So, there were several Disciples outside Englewood who had their own leaders.

David Barksdale became the leader of the Devil's Disciple at the height of many activities in the Hyde Park and Kenwood neighborhoods. Around the same period, the University of Chicago supported a program to renovate the Southern Kenwood and Northern Hyde Park. This would lead to the clearing of slum buildings and renovation of the homes that could be salvaged. This project ultimately increased property value in these neighborhoods and consequently sent the impoverished Black communities moving to nearby Englewood. As more families moved into Englewood, the Devil's Disciple grew strong in number and presence and set up their new headquarters at 63rd Normal in 1963. The University of Chicago project led to the demolition of several houses around 53rd and Kimbark in Hyde Park; consequently, shopping plazas were built on what used to be headquarters for Disciples.

Sometime in 1964 at 68th and Green Englewood, a group of young black boys, primarily teenagers, gathered at Larry Hoover's home and watched through the window as gangsters and pimps hung out in the parking lot of Guys and Gals Night Club. These teenagers desired to be like those gangsters and pimps. At the time, they were located between two rival street gangs, the Rangers and the Disciples. Larry Hoover hatched the idea of forming their club, and he followed up by starting to dress like a gang leader from that day.

Although he was not the leader at first, Larry would be credited for naming the "Supreme Gangsters." Larry enjoyed working behind the scenes while he teamed up with a street hustler, Andrew Howard, known on the streets as "Dee Dee," and Ike Taylor, also known as "King Ike," as his right-hand man. The Supreme Gangster chose a unique way of greeting each other with a clenched fist instead of a regular handshake. Their symbol is a crowned heart with wings and a sword pierced through the heart. Their color is predominantly black.

Since it was formed, the Supreme Gangsters had no beef with the Disciples, but they were constantly at war with the Egyptian Cobras and the Blackstone Rangers. As the new gang in the neighborhood, the Blackstone Rangers targeted the Supreme Gangster to try to flush them out before they became more formidable and gained more territories. Unlike the Disciples, Blackstone Rangers, and other gangs who focused on street territorial dominance, the Supreme Gangsters were about business and money. They set clear goals to make sure their members were aligned.

Larry Hoover was barely thirteen when the Supreme Gangster was formed, and by age 14, in 1965, there was a leadership vacuum in the Supreme Gangster gang which meant Hoover had to step up to the helm. Under his leadership, the group recruited older members who had more than high school qualifications. The gang won more street battles against the Blackstone Rangers and grew exponentially in

Englewood, getting the attention of other more prominent gangs and the authorities.

The Blackstone Rangers were better organized than the Disciples. They were always in the news because they worked with some agencies and had sponsors in government quarters. The argument of who had more members between Disciples and Blackstone Rangers will always be there.

In 1996, the Disciples felt the Rangers were using their various influences to recruit more members. During this time, Larry Hoover and David Barksdale, young men of about the same age, agreed to merge their gangs to form a formidable force. To counter these movements and threats from the Rangers, David Barksdale also absorbed many small gangs in the South Side that had equal beef with the Rangers. This coalition against a common enemy led to the creation of the "Black Disciple Nation." Eventually, the Disciples expanded further into Southside neighborhoods like Washington Park, Woodlawn, Greater Grand Crossing, and other black communities. Both Larry and David became "Kings" and ran the group together. This is where the name "King David," and "King Larry" came about.

For someone so notorious and feared in Chicago and everywhere gangs existed, David Barksdale's official records show he was not a drug dealer, nor a killer. He was barely ever convicted for a few crimes. As the King of the Disciples, one would expect his record to be filled with felonies. However, from his rap sheet, you can tell he was just a regular street hustler who committed petty crimes. Unlike Hoover, who was about the business and money, and Jeff Ford (leader of the Rangers), who was about power and control, David seemed to be a regular street guy. Although not all criminals are arrested for every major crime they commit- maybe he was a dangerous man who was never arrested for those crimes.

David Barksdale was arrested more than 25 times in his lifetime. According to 2008 research by the National Gang Crime Research

Center, David Barksdale used multiple aliases during his numerous arrests. Below are King David's official criminal records, leader of the most prominent black street gang in the history of American street gangs.

- The rap sheet begins with the arrest of David Jones, 5 May 1965, for Criminal Trespass to Vehicle. Judge Comerford dismissed this case.
- On 13 July 1965, the arrest was for "Resisting Arrest," and on 28 July 1965, "Resisting Arrest and Disorderly Conduct." The case also went to Judge Comerford.
- The first twist on the actual name begins on 2 December 1965, "David L. Barksdale," with an investigation for Aggravated Battery.
- The following alias (Davis Jones) comes on 31 December 1966 for Strong Arm Robbery. He gives a home address of 8407 S. Morgan.
- Arrested as Davis L. Barksdale 14 February 1967 for Burglary, released without charge, and listed as living at 522 W. 64th Street.
- He was arrested then again on 26 April 1967 as Donise Barksdale for Assault and Resisting Arrest. It was non-suited—address given: 6452 S. Union.
- An entry on 10 August 1967 for David L. Barksdale (6452 S. Union) indicates "Appl. Chicago Urban Oppt.", which presumably means an anti-gang program or gang-treatment program.
- David Barksdale was arrested on 13 September 1967 for Possession of Marijuana, but Judge Wendt dismissed the case.
- George Walker was an alias used in the arrest on 13 October 1967 for Disorderly Conduct. Still, again the charge was non-suited (Judge Wendt again).
- David L. Barksdale, on 1 February 1968, was arrested for Resisting and Disorderly Conduct (Xparte $25, Judge Cerda).

- On 7 April 1968, David Barksdale was arrested for curfew, but the case was dismissed (Judge Lee).
- On 28 May 1968, David L. Barksdale was arrested for Aggravated Assault, Battery, and Criminal Property Damage. Again, the case was dismissed by Judge Cerda.
- On 8 June 1968, David Barksdale was arrested for Disorderly Conduct (Xparte $25 & N.C., Judge Zelezinski)
- David D. Barksdale was arrested on 27 June 1968 for mob action. Again on 3 July 1968 for Aggravated Battery.
- Arrested 24 July 1968 for warrants on the two prior arrests, received six months in the "House of Corrections" (i.e., today known as Cook County Jail) by Judge Zelezinski.
- On 3 August 1968, he was charged with Criminal Damage to Property, but on 3 November 1968, it was dismissed (Judge Zelezinski).
- Similarly, on 4 August 1968, David Barksdale was charged with Resisting Arrest and Disorderly Conduct. Once again, the case was dismissed by Judge Zelezinski.
- He was arrested on 7 March 1969 for a Battery Warrant. Judge Zelezinski dismissed the case.
- Again, on 4 September 1969, he was brought in for "Mob Action." Again dismissed (S.O.L., Judge Genesen).
- He was arrested on 14 August 1969 for unlawful use of a weapon and defacing I.D. Judge Mooney dismissed the case.
- Arrested on 15 January 1970 for intimidation, dismissed (S.O.L., Judge Hechinger).
- David Lee Barksdale was arrested for Resisting Arrest on 7 May 1970. He was discharged on 10 March 1971 by Judge Genesen.
- David was again arrested on 4 September 1970 for mob action, held to the grand jury (Judge Dunne). He was indicted for Mob Action by the Grand Jury. Verdict: not guilty (Judge Aspen).
- On 9 January 1971, David was arrested for defacing firearms and discharging a weapon. He gets six months in the county jail (Judge Dunne).

- The next record entry is 12 January 1971, for traffic court.
- He was arrested on 26 January 1971 for armed robbery conspiracy, dismissed by Judge Murphy. A 21 June 71 entry for traffic court.
- There was a blank entry for 11 July 1972 in the 6th district (C.B. No. 3586047).
- On 18 January 1974, John David Barksdale was arrested for Gambling (dice). Judge Neal dismissed the case.

Finally, on 13 February 1974, for possession of marijuana and fictitious license plates. He was sentenced to 3 days in jail and a $100 fine by Judge Murphy.

Shooting and Death

David Barksdale assumed the Devil's Disciple's leadership until he died, and he worked to merge or absorb the smaller gangs to form a formidable force. Between 1968 and 1970, he worked relentlessly to broker peace with the Black P. Stones, but failed. In June 1970, King David was shot while chilling with his buddy Larry Hoover at a bar in the Englewood neighborhood. The shooters were members of the Black P. Stones gang. Larry acted quickly by rushing Barksdale to a nearby hospital. Doctors discovered that an M-14 bullet had passed through his kidney, causing severe damage.

Although he was shot six times, he survived the shooting, but Barksdale was never the same again, because his health started failing him from that point. Investigation revealed that the leader of the Black Stone Rangers, Eugene Hairston, had ordered the shooting by "commissioning" several teenagers to kill Barksdale.

There are conflicting records as to exactly how King David Barksdale finally died. One report said he died from the effect of the 1970 shooting that affected his kidney and caused it to deteriorate over time. Another record said that though he was never the same after the shooting, an accidental discharge from a teenage gang member dealt the final blow.

King David was survived by his wife, Yvonne "Cookie" Barksdale, and three children, David Jr, Melinda, and Ronnie, who were twins. Even after his death, his family was not spared from the gang life. His wife, Yvonne, was murdered in 1977, and one of his children was also killed in 1996 by the Gangster Disciples.

Legacy

The Black Disciples still revere Barksdale to this day and hold an annual posthumous birthday in his honor. For example, in 2008, a parade sponsored and supported by the Black Disciples was registered by the Chicago City Council to be held during Memorial Day Weekend. This move was heavily criticized by the Fraternal Order of Police, citing concerns about the potential of an outbreak of gang violence.

Depending on who is talking about it, David Barkdales's legacy has always been shrouded in controversy. Despite being the first black man to control the largest gang in American history, some would say his legacy is that of blood-shedding, law-breaking, and violence. They believe there is no reason to revere him in any way, mainly because he claims that he lined up 100 people and clubbed them to death using a golf club.

This claim does not appear on the list of indictments in police records, even with all the aliases he used.

David Barksdale was indeed a notorious gang leader of the most prominent street gang ever, but he also used his power to impact his community positively. For example, in 1966, when the Black Disciples became a "nation," they became heavily involved in community service, opened legitimate businesses, ran fundraisers, and enforced school policies to keep kids in school. The Disciples had ties with civil rights groups and joined in protesting against injustices-fighting for the rights of Black American, impoverished neighborhoods. Although some of the funds raised might have gone into illegal activities like drugs and firearms, the Black Disciples and the Gangster Disciples did a lot to invest in their communities.

In 1967, the Disciples and the Rangers partnered with the government in the Chicago Job Campaign. The Woodlawn Organization was awarded more than $927,000 to be shared between the two rival gangs for job training for the young people in the Woodlawn neighborhood. Both gang leaders were paid salaries to serve as instructors in this program, even though the majority of them lacked formal education. Barksdale's Disciples received $360,000 as their share of the program.

Today's Drill rappers from Chicago and beyond are singing, talking, and honoring King David for his contribution to the street struggles. Many still see him as a leader, and they respect him in the way they can.

The story of David Barksdale is about a young man who lived and died on the street. Though he was not formally educated, he created a system of leadership that allowed other gang leaders to be who they wanted to be and still be Disciples. King David will probably go down in history as the only gang leader with no significant crime linked to him besides petty ones.

Whichever side of the divide you are on, you will admit that he was a unique gentleman who will forever be talked about when it comes to struggling on the street and living in impoverished neighborhoods.

In subsequent chapters, you will read more about his relationship with Larry Hoover and how they ran the streets.

Chapter Three

Biography

Larry Hoover was born on November 25 1950 in Jackson, Mississippi. His parents moved to Chicago, Illinois, when he was just four years old. The family is made up of his siblings, parents, and grandparents. Larry was not an educated young man when he took to life on the street.

Larry Hoover, the stuttering young man from Mississippi, would later become one of the biggest names in gangster history, not just in America but in the world.

Growing Up in Chicago

Larry Hoover faced some challenges while growing up. He once said in an interview that his mother was quite strict, but she did not know he was part of a gang until he was shot the third time.

As a young man, he was always trying to make a buck. He once sold Jet Magazine on "el" mass transit; he carried groceries and cleaned furnaces as part of his early struggles to make some money. Despite all those efforts, the family still relied on State Welfare. So, whatever he could not buy, he stole. He would steal clothes and hide them with a friend, then change into them before walking to school. Hoover was never satisfied with whatever his mother could afford to provide.

Schooling was another challenging period in Hoover's life. While in Francis Parker High School, he loved and played basketball and did very well in math. Maybe that explains where he got his business acumen and why he ran the Gangster Disciples like a business enterprise. A former school counselor described Hoover as an above-average student who sweated a lot whenever he was asked to read because he stuttered and the other kids made fun of him.

Larry Hoover was involved in one gang fight too many, leading to the end of his quest for formal education. On his first day in another school, a rival gang member shot him in the thigh right outside the principal's office. It seemed too much for the school to handle, so Hoover was expelled. However, back on the street, Hoover felt adequate and loved; he felt nobody could prey on him because he belonged to a brotherhood and a family.

Often, he enjoyed hanging out with his girlfriend and another buddy of his, Wallace Bradley. Their favorite joints were the South Side nightclubs like Guys and Gals and the Green Bunny. He was always known to be a good dresser who had a good carriage.

Larry Hoover was popularly known as "King Larry," "Prince Larry," "The King of Kings," and "The Honorable Chairman." He was part of the "Supreme Gangster" founding members that later metamorphosed into the "Supreme Gangster Disciples." After the merger arrangement with his late buddy David Barksdale, Hoover was made a co-leader of the "Black Gangster Disciple Nation" with David.

Hoover is currently serving six life imprisonment sentences at the ADX Florence Super Maximum Prison, Colorado. After the death of his friend David and the eventual breakup of the various gangs that he merged with, Hoover's group took up the name Gangster Disciples (GD). The GD is known to be involved in criminal activities on the streets they controlled and in other areas, including extortion, money laundering, conspiracy, shootings,, assaults, etc.

Furthermore, under Hoover's control, the Gangster Disciples got involved in the illegal drug trade on the street and in the prisons. Their activities started from the West Side and extended through many streets across the United States. King Larry was barely twelve years old when he got involved in street gang life and criminal activities. As he assumed the leadership of GD, his illegal activities increased exponentially. These days, while still serving his life term, Larry has been busy trying to clean up the image of the Gangster Disciples saying the "GD" actually means "Growth and Development."

In 1969, when Hoover assumed complete control of the group, he grew the South Side of the gang and improved on their drug deals. It was estimated that under Hoover's leadership, the group raked in up to $1,000 daily from drug deal back then.

Some people believed Hoover was David Barksdale's henchman. This is the general conclusion in the Police force. They thought he was responsible for far more shootings than accounted for. For his part, Hoover said, he just loved the guy, wanted him as a mentor, he emulated his charisma, and chose to follow him.

Hoover was on David Barksdale's side when they were both exposed to political activism. Under the leadership of Barksdale and Hoover, gang members mobilized and rallied behind Martin Luther King Jr's open-housing march on the white community of Marquette Park. Furthermore, in 1969, the Disciples, Vice Lords, and Rangers rallied behind another civil rights movement. This time, it was a campaign to shut down construction projects and pressure Chicago building unions to hire more Blacks against the 97% white they employed.

By the time he was twenty years old, Hoover had been in and out of prison several times for different offenses. He had also survived several assassination attempts. On record, he survived more than six shooting orders on his life by rival gangs.

Under Hoover's leadership, the Gangster Disciples were vicious and ruthless. You could get drilled for the most insignificant offense. They were known to even kill their members for issues such as disrespect and stealing. This was the case with William "Pooky" Young.

The Murder of William "Pooky" Young

After the death of David Barksdale, Hoover took complete charge of the Black Gangster Disciples Nation (BGDN), and invariably he had complete control of the drug trade. Using his influence and power, the BGDN won over more rival gangs and forged a merger with groups like the Ambrose Two-Two Boys, Satan's Disciple, La Roza Nation, Simon City Royals, Imperial Gangsters, Harrison Gents, Maniac Latin Disciples, North Side Insane Popes, Latin Eagles, Spanish Gangster Disciples, and Spanish Cobras.

However, in 1989, the BGDN started having internal crises over drug deals. The fight was more between the Black Disciples and the Gangster Disciples over drug sales in the Englewood neighborhood in Chicago. The internal problems degenerated quickly into violence, which led to the deaths of several members of the BDGN.. Eventually, the conflict led to the breakup of the Black Gangster Disciples Nation and created two arch-rivals, the Black Disciples and the Gangster Disciples. For many years, these rival groups attacked each with hundreds of lives lost, another hundred languishing in various jails, and many lives and property destroyed.

The Black Disciples, which David Barksdale formed, was not originally under the control of Hoover, and he was not involved in their activities, at least not until the death of Barksdale. However, Hoover was involved with the gang organization of the Devil's Disciples.

The Gangster Disciples that exist till this day as an arch-rival to the Black Disciples have been called several names in the course of their metamorphosis. These names include the Family, Supreme Gangster, Black Gangsters Disciples (BGDs), Black Gangster Disciple Nation (BGDN), but the Gangster is the most consistent one of the names, mainly because it was formed after the forged alliance failed and while Hoover was in prison serving his sentence for the murder of William "Pookey" Young.

Before the breakup, there was a significant event that rocked the foundation of the BGDN to its foundation and forced some drastic changes. In February 1973, Larry Hoover discovered that some gang members were stealing from the group. One of them was identified as William "Pookey" Young, who was only 19 years old at that time. He was also a resident of the neighborhood. On 26 February, 1973, Hoover ordered three other gang members to hunt and kill William. He was abducted and shot dead with his body dumped in an alley near 68th street and Union Avenue in the Englewood, Chicago neighborhood.

One of the gang members who carried out the order of shooting William was Andrew Howard. Consequently, on March 16 1973, the police arrested Larry Hoover, the gang leader, and Andrew Howard. Both men were charged with the murder of William "Pooky" Young. In November that same year, they were sentenced to 150 to 200 years in prison.

When he was sentenced to serve his time at the Stateville Maximum Security Prison, 20 miles Southwest of Chicago in Joliet, his wife was pregnant with their son.

The Bars Could Not Stop Larry Hoover

When he was sentenced to 150 to 200 years, one would have thought that would be the end of his criminal activities and ultimately the death of the street gang he ran. After all, the prison was supposed to serve as a correctional facility where inmates are reformed to be better people before re-joining society. However, in the case of Larry Hoover, the outcome was different. The prison didn't reform him. He became even more vicious, and his influence from behind bars grew beyond the imagination of the authorities.

In 1976, Hoover flexed his influence and organized a work stoppage at the Stateville to protest bad food. He was later transferred to another prison in Pontiac. Within three months of his arrival there, a riot broke out , leading to the death of three prison officials. Many people from within and outside the facility pointed their fingers at Larry Hoover as the mastermind of the whole thing. Hoover was indicted. The charges were later dropped for lack of evidence; moreover, no one was willing to step forward and testify against Larry Hoover at that time. Such was the type of influence Hoover had.

In 1979, one inmate, "Nissan," an original member of the Devil's Disciple, carried out an assassination attempt against Hoover. The attempt involved using a gay fellow inmate to stab Hoover, but the attempt failed, and the gay prisoner died violently.

While still serving his time, sometime around the 80s, Hoover was transferred to a minimum-security facility where he had unrestricted access to visitors and phones, which allowed him to communicate with the outside world. Hoover started running complex gang operations from behind bars. He could reach out to the low-ranking street officers in the gang within Chicago and other cities, streets, and neighborhoods. He was referred to as the "Chairman of the Board".

There was the exchange of professionally written memos from Hoover to several of the rank and file of the organization. It remains unclear if Hoover wrote some of the directives or if the gang had a well-learned secretary who produced the content of these memos with the approval of the "Chairman of the Board".

During this period, Hoover was in charge of the Gangster Disciples' drug trade operations in the South and near Chicago's West Side and quickly expanded drug sales throughout America. He added a couple of gangs to his alliance in these expansions, including the Spanish Gangster Disciples, La Raza Nation, Black Disciples, and Maniac Latin Disciples.

In the following years, inmates started looking to Hoover to offer them protection in exchange for loyalty; they were recruited as devotee Gangster Disciples. On the other hand, the wardens also recognized his influence, and they trusted him to keep the inmates calm and prevent any form of uprising in prison.

At the time of his sentencing in 1974, Hoover was diagnosed as functionally illiterate. He would later claim that he had never read any book in his life, not even a comic book. However, Hoover worked on and fixed that weakness by studying and earning a high school diploma. He followed through by reading a wide range of books about different topics. Some of his all-time favorite books are Machiavelli's "The Prince," "The Fountainhead" by Ayn Rand, and "Boss" written by the former mayor of Chicago. The last book particularly inspired him because he believed he could transition the Gangster Disciples from a violent street gang to a socially acceptable gang, as seen in some white and Irish gangs in Chicago in the 1900s.

Some of these books played a pivotal role in Larry Hoover's transformation agenda. In an enigmatic manner, Hoover started sharing his "New Vision" among gang members through a 45-page manifesto-like plan known as "The Blueprint." part of the content revealed how Hoover urged his gang members to pay more attention to educating themselves, to learn more about business, shun crime, and to be part of a political movement to shape their community. He would later say in his words about the "New Vision" and plan, "It was a combination of getting older and seeing all these kids come into the system. These kids needed help, and if I wasn't going to help them, who would?" Below are a couple of his notes.

"We have found ourselves gangbanging, shooting, and killing each other. We are byproducts of the same era that produced the gangster era. The answer to our problems cannot be found in carbon Al Capone, rather our approach to society's injustices must become innovative, and creative."

While spreading the news of the change to his soldiers on the streets across the United States, Hoover also changed the gang's name from "Gangster Disciples" to "Growth and Development". He followed that by replacing his title of "King" with a more business-related one,

"Chairman," while at the same time setting up a "Board of Directors" of inmates.

According to Hoover, he dissociated himself from the gangster Disciples' drug dealings and all devices, but he never stepped down as the head of the group. Hoover felt he would lose people he was reaching out to if he started a new group. Meanwhile, GD and Hoover's influence was multiplying in the early 80s thanks to the early release program in Illinois releasing many gang members back into the Chicago neighborhood. The gang network widened, and communication became a lot easier because members were going in and out of prison.

Figures from law enforcement say the Gangster Disciples' soldiers grew to as many as 30,000 and spread across 35 states, and out of the 38,000 men in prison, 12,000 to 20,000 were GDs. It was also alleged that the GD had infiltrated the corrections officers and the Chicago Police Department.

In 1987, Larry Hoover was transferred to a minimum-security prison in Vienna. The Vienna facility had no fence; it was a college-like atmosphere. This arrangement made it easy for Hoover to keep in touch with the street. He went shopping one day and had several visitors, many of whom were fellow GD members. By the 90s, with the confidence that he could make a strong case and get paroled, he made what many will see as the riskiest decision of his life by launching the Gangster Disciples into Chicago politics while still incarcerated.

By 1990, Hoover started the 21st Century VOTE. In 1993 an Englewood group started involving GD members in political protests in City Hall, community cleanups, and voter registration drives. A year later, GD supported unsuccessful candidates, one of which had links with Hoover. He was an old schoolmate, Hal Baskin, and the other was Gator Bradley. In a telephone recorded conversation with the leader of the disciples, Hoover, was quoted as saying about the election, "See it's 40% African vote in Chicago and that is our folks.

That is folks in the projects, the poor people." In the same phone conversation, Hoover referred to the 21st century as his "Political Action Committee."

Hoover's profile got a further boost. In 1993, he sent a pre-recorded speech to a picnic gathering of 10,000 GD members and supporters in rural Kankakee County. He used his influence to push for a citywide "peace summit" and a wide range of community programs. Some of these included gang deactivation and after-school sports, mainly in Englewood High School.

At his 1993 and 1995 parole hearings, Larry Hoover gained the support of some prominent Chicago people. For example, the former mayor Eugene Sawyer, church ministers, academics, and more than 40,000 Gang members signed a petition organized by the 21st Century Vote. In 1994, Hoover was transferred back to Vienna on his request, his freedom seemed imminent, and his fame grew stronger.

At about 4 a.m. on 31 August 1995, Hoover was called out to the warden's office and taken away by federal officers who came armed and prepared in unmarked cars. He was flown out to Chicago Meigs field, where a federal judge told him he was being indicted on drug conspiracy charges that carried mandatory death sentences without the possibility of parole. Hoover was shocked as he pled not guilty.

At the same time, more than 250 federal agents swept through the South Side in search of more than 38 gang members who had visited Hoover while he was in prison. Most of them were top GD leaders. According to a police report, Larry Hoover was living a luxurious lifestyle and running a Gangster Disciple operation from the Vienna prison. His phone conversations with GD leaders were recorded, proving that Hoover used the 21st Century Vote as a means of money laundering and narcotics trades. Furthermore, informants indicated that the proceeds from the non-profit organization, 21st Century Vote, did not go to the poor; instead, the funds were diverted for money laundering. Among the GD leaders arrested, quite a number of them were convicted.

In a campaign for Hoover's freedom, his wife managed the recording and sale of a Drill rap with T-shirts bearing Hoover's picture with the inscription, "Free All Political Prisoners". As part of efforts to gather further support, "The Blueprint" was published.

Meanwhile, on the streets, especially among gang members, it was believed that the officers were corrupt and wanted to keep Hoover locked up to die in prison because they were afraid of his influence if released. On the other hand, federal officers believed Hoover's good intentions were a mere ploy to get himself out of prison to continue his illegal activities. According to them, the GDs were fast increasing in number and spreading across the country. At the same time, sales and profits from the GD drug trade were rising into millions of dollars.

Finally, in 1997, Larry Hoover was found guilty of all charges and sentenced to six life sentences. He is currently serving time at the ADX Florence, Colorado.

During an interview with The Christian Science Monitor, Larry Hoover talked about a wide range of topics. Here are a few quotes from him about some issues.

About Prison Life

"You become more conscious in prison - of life, of community, of your own mortality - so you better understand the need for survival. You don't just see what's happening to you, you see why it's happening, and can start thinking about making changes to make sure it doesn't happen to you and your offspring in the future."

On Political Activism

"I realized that these street gangs could be the salvation of the community because street gangs were at the core of most of the negative things going on... If the leadership would start thinking positive, then they could redirect that negative energy and become a viable part of the community."

"You can't deal with street organizations from the outside... I've been out there, I've done everything they have. I've robbed and been shot ... so they can relate to me."

About Drug Dealing

"Most gang members sell drugs because there ain't no jobs out there... It's doing a job, puttin' food on the table."

On Plans to Start a Union

"My plan was to bring all the street organizations together and form a street organization union, collecting a dollar a week dues ... that would be $1.2 million to $2.4 million a year ... then we could get together and form a company that would manufacture gym shoes with the United in Peace symbol on the gym shoes. And those shoes would sell, because they are coming out of Chicago and Chicago is looked at as the gang capital of the country."

About Chicago Politics

"[Chicago's political machine] can't control the apathetic vote, and that's what I was advocating that we wake up - street gang members, people who live in the projects, homeless... Mayor Daley is afraid of me because he understands the potential of the type of movement I'm trying to push..."

"I think 21st Century VOTE was my best effort, and my most costly effort - it motivated these indictments."

On Secret Tape Recordings

"I think [federal] tapes [of his conversations] were sliced up and put together... If all 65 hours were transcribed, it would show exculpatory evidence."

On his organization's future, if he was convicted.

"I could see it floundering, because any time there's a movement, you need a head. Without central leadership, I can see my move to galvanize youth most likely take the same turn as the civil rights movement took in the 1960s."

Business Structure

For a man who was declared functionally illiterate when going to jail, Hoover did well to change his educational status, later creating a complex administration style for running the gang. If you come across some of the flow charts and memos used in managing the gang's affairs, you will be forgiven for assuming they are from a standard corporate organization. However, they also clearly show that Hoover was a micro-manager.

Below is an example of how Hoover managed the Gangster Disciple like a business enterprise.

	Role	Appointed BY	Responsibilities
1	Chairman of the Board	Self	Responsible for the gang and approves several decisions before they are carried out.
2	Board of Directors	Chairman	They establish policies and amend National laws. Policy approval and education of the national body Listen to all complaints from all members of the Gangster Disciple Nation.
3	Institutional Coordinators	Chairman	There is one for each prison institution. They, in turn, appoint Unit Coordinators, more like Cellhouse Leaders. The unit coordinators oversee the activities of the gang and report to their Institutional coordinators. They ensure enforcement of all GD laws and policies and report to the Chairman about the functional progress of the gang.

4	Institutional Secretaries	Chairman	They are responsible for all the literature and correspondences for the GD nation. They screen all incoming and outgoing members. They operate as the emissary of the Board of Directors and report to the Chairman daily.
5	Institutional Legal Coordinator	Chairman	Oversee all legal affairs of the gang, which include complaints, grievances, functions of the gang, and reports.
6	Educational Program Directors	Chairman	They oversee teaching within the institution to GD members. Lead classes and quizzes on GD literature and report daily to the Chairman on the functions and progress of the teaching staff.
7	Institutional Exercise Coordinator	Chairman	In charge of all sporting activities and social events within the group. Ensures the daily and weekly exercises routines are carried out and reported to the Chairman.

| 8 | Institutional Treasurer | Chairman | Appoints Unit Treasurers who oversee the nation's finances, render weekly reports to the Chairman of the Board. |

Under the leadership of Hoover, some rules governed the affairs of the group in and out of prison. For instance, in 1981, LHoover issued a memo to his troops saying, "No Gangster Disciple can ever assault, threaten or disrespect a correctional officer without his "blessing." Threatening or assaulting a correctional officer would amount to a serious "violation" of the GD rules. This memo became one of the 16 rules by which Hoover ran the prison operation, and all members had to abide by them. The gang members followeyd the rule, and it consequently earned Hoover some favor. This was the reason that he was rewarded with the transfer to the Vienna, Illinois, minimum-security facility where he lived a luxurious life and had unrestricted communication with the outside world.

Hoover issued several memos before his arrest and prosecution by the federal agents. Below are some samples showing the structure of the directives and how they were constructed.

These memos were obtained from the National Gang Crime Research Center website, and no attempts have been made to correct the grammar, spelling, and punctuations. Also, the memos are not in any particular sequence.

Memo. 1:

The Oct. 1, 1981, Typed Memo From Larry Hoover to His GD Troops

Date: October 1, 1981

From: The Chairman, Co-Chairman, and the Board of Directors.

To: All Brothers of the Struggle.

The Chairman and the Board of Directors wish to extend our love, Life, and loyalty to all Brothers of the Struggle! We are pleased with the support and participation of many of you who have helped us transition from the Old to the New.

Many of you have a copy of the Organization's <u>Preface</u>. The Preface explains the New Concept and the direction that the organization has taken. As we stated in the Preface, "In the process of going from the Old to the New, we will have a few complications." As predicted, we have had our share of complications, but we refuse to allow anyone or anything to stagnate our progress or expansion. In spite of the few complications, we are happy to report that we are making progress. In order for us as an Organization to continue to progress and expand, we must become more <u>educated</u>, <u>politically motivated</u> and aware of the <u>economical realities</u> of Black America.

Laws and Sentences have become more stiffer and longer and more prisons are being built with us in mind. We as an Organization of young Black Men cannot allow ourselves to stay confined behind walls and locked in cages to slowly grow old and useless. Through <u>Business</u> and <u>Politics</u>, we can build an economical base that will insure us boundless power and wealth. But if we stay uneducated and without political power, prisons and death will continue to be a way of life for many of us.

<u>Now</u> is the time to put down the Donald Goins books. It is time for us to pick up the <u>business</u>, <u>law</u>, <u>political</u> and <u>economical books</u>. It is time for us to go to school, learn trades and develop all of our talents and skills, so that we will become stronger in society. We cannot wait for the system to teach us, we must take it upon ourselves to learn all that we can about this world. We must not be afraid to change or grow. We, as an Organization will not stand still and die.

All Brothers are to have a copy of the Preface and the Laws of the Organization, these papers are to be kept at all times, they are for you to study and learn. These papers are important and should be treated as such. From time to time, you will be requested to attend and participate in meetings to read and discuss all documents that has been issued to the membership. It is important that you as a member of the Organization, know exactly what the Organization is about and where it is going.

Many of us are unassigned, it is important that all of us have assignments. We need to be everywhere, capitalizing on the learning experience and the profits that each assignment has to offer.

Everyone will be required to fill out an application. The reason for the application is for the Chairman and his Board of Directors to know more about you and help place you in a program or assignment that will best suit you as an individual and as a member of this Organization.

Some of our brothers have been indicted for murder. We are to give these Brothers all of our support. We encourage you to help in any way that you can. If they are found guilty, they will face the electric chair. We as an Organization will do all that we can to see that they are free.

Many of the Laws that govern our Organization are still being disregarded and disrespected. All Laws are to be adhered to and respected. Those that continue to disregard and disrespect the laws of this Organization will be violated and eradicated (removed) from this Organization.

Again, Thanks for your cooperation and participation.

SINCERELY,

CHAIRMAN AND BOARD OF DIRECTORS

Memo. 2:

Larry Hoover

DIXON CORRECTIONAL CENTER

2600 North Brinton

P.O. Box 1200

Dixon, Illinois 61021

My Brothers and Sisters in the Struggle:

I learned this week, for the 13th time, that I have once again been denied parole. My thoughts, as they have been for years now, are of my family and of you. My sons, who have grown from infants to men during my imprisonment, and their mother, whose commitment has been unwavering: they all continue to pay, with me, the price for the terrible crime I committed, for which I am solely and fully responsible. They have been strong, as the families of tens of thousands of other black prisoners have been and must be strong every day of their lives.

But, Brothers and Sisters, we must have more than strength. We must have vision, too. We must see that we, ourselves, are the victims of the crimes that ignorance, poverty, hopelessness and drugs lead us to commit. We must see that, just as no man is an island, we all wear the shackles of the ghetto. We are all Ghetto Prisoners.

Our only hope for release is to use our strength and vision in the cause of change. Ignorance is our enemy; we must honor learning and those who learn. Poverty is our enemy; we must gather our pennies and dollars and use them in our own communities. Hopelessness is our enemy; we must organize and vote by the hundreds of thousands, to give voice to the voiceless. Drugs are our enemy, destroying many of us with the lure of profit, more of us with addiction, and still more with the crime that results; we must join our voices with those across the land, of whites and blacks, churchgoers and convicts, gays and straights - all who share the purpose of taking the profit out of drugs and ending the slaughter made easy by guns.

Whether and when I will be released is beyond my control. Whatever my personal destiny may be, I will fight to strike the shackles that imprison us all.

(signed)

Larry Hoover

Ghetto Prisoner #1829

Memo. 3:

TO:ALL BROTHERS OF THE STRUGGLE

FR:BOARD OF DIRECTORS

DT:JULY 20, 1991

RE: PLAN OF ACTION

"HOW TO STRENGTHEN OUR ORGANIZATION"

What can I do to put new life into our organization? This is a question countless of thousands of us are asking. Groups or associations are in constant need for renewal from within. This applies whether they be civic, religious, educational, business, labor, political, fraternal or any other type of organization.

It is up to thousands of rank and file members to realize that the continued renewal of our organization is the business of each and everyone of us. These considerations may enable you to do your part:

1) <u>ATTEND MEETINGS REGULARLY</u>. Make it a matter of principle to attend meetings regularly. You can't participate unless you are physically present. Be more than just one of the folks. If you think an organization is worth joining, then it deserves your personal, intelligent, active and continuing support. Don't stay away from meetings because they are not ran the way you think they should be. Strive to improve them and encourage them, and encourage others to do the same. Remember you have no right to complain about the nations business, if you don't attend meetings.

2) <u>KEEP IN MIND THE PURPOSE OF OUR ORGANIZATION</u>. Any organization can lose sight of it's objectives and drift into side issues. So occasionally review the concept and laws, as well as the operating procedures for the nation, (i.e., policies, past/present decisions made by the leadership, etc.). Also, encourage others to do the same, as well as stick to the goals of the "<u>BLACK GANGSTER DISCIPLE NATION</u>". If the goals of the nation appear outdated, make steps to up-date them.

3) <u>LIVE UP TO THE DUTIES OF MEMBERSHIP</u>. These are the marks of a real G.D.:

a. He/she willingly fulfills the responsibilities that goes with his/her rights.

b. He/she knows that what he/she does or leaves undone helps or hurts everyone.

c. He/she realize the limitations of a G.D., but does what is reasonably expected of him/her.

d. He/she opens their ears to listen, as well as their mouths to speak.

4) <u>SHOW A PERSONAL INTEREST</u>. Nation business can become quite cold and impersonal unless all brothers of the struggle go out of their way to inject a personal note to everything they do. Try to be in harmony instead of being distant or hostile. Blend gentleness with firmness when you must take a stand. Respect the viewpoint and feelings of others no matter how much you may differ.

5) <u>THINK FOR YOURSELF</u>. It takes effort to be a thinker instead of a yes man. Unless you take some initiative you may be depriving yourself, as well as others of the benefits of the knowledge you secretly possess. Study the various aspects of issues so that you can make a judgement on your own. Base your views on reasons, principles, personalities and on the common good; not emotions or narrow partisanship.

6) <u>DEVELOP YOUR ABILITY TO COMMUNICATE</u>. More than one organization has been saved from an embarrassing decision by the voice of a lone individual who stood up and made his voice heard. Know what you are talking about in the first place. Unlock your own powers of leadership and everyone will profit.

7) <u>MOST IMPORTANT, DEVELOP AND PROMOTE A SPIRIT OF TOGETHERNESS</u>. Our nation has been crippled by the lack of leadership, as well as members forming uncooperative or hostile cliques. There is always hope! Even one person, by fair mindness and objectivity can bridge the gap between opposing sides. The "Chairman" will truly bless you if you have any hand in bringing this nation back together again and upholding the laws of the "<u>BLACK GANGSTER DISCIPLE NATION</u>".

8) <u>SEEK THE BEST INTEREST OF EVERYONE</u>. This is a double barreled point.

a. It means ensuring that all members and not just a few share the benefits of the nation; and

b. It involves taking into account the interest of the nation at large, and not just a few of the folks.

9) <u>ACT WISE AT ALL TIMES</u>. When misunderstandings arise, as well as disputes and clashes. You can help by trying to reach a peaceful accord. You may *not completely succeed simply because talking about it isn't always the solution to the problem.*

10) GIVE CREDIT WHERE CREDIT IS DUE. Many "Brothers of the Struggle" are annoying "Credit Grabbers", who are the first in line when it comes to taking a bow. On the other hand, nowhere to be found when responsibility must be shared. If you are truly concerned with the continued success of the nation. Regardless of who gets the praise, you will be giving no small service to the nation. Don't hesitate to praise a fellow member for a job well done. Your continuing effort to give praise will make this organization that much stronger and work that much smoother.

11) PREVENT SENSELESS MEETINGS. Whenever a meeting is to take place. Help keep things moving by making a clear distinction between essentials and nonessentials because of time limitations. Only matters of importance; practical and relevant should be proposed. Persuade capable people to seek positions. Point out to individuals with the capacity and motivation what great good they could do the nation by serving in positions of leadership. Find out before hand their qualifications and act on the basis of such qualifications; not personal loyalty or selfish advantages.

12) GIVE YOUR LEADERS RESPECT AND COOPERATION. Even if someone is calling shots whom you don't personally like. They represent you, as well as the "BLACK GANGSTER DISCIPLE NATION". They should receive the support you would expect if you were in that position.

13) OFFER CONSTRUCTIVE SUGGESTIONS. Don't tell them only what you think they want to hear. On the other hand, don't keep bringing up senseless complaints. Speak well of your leaders to outsiders. If you don't have nothing good to say about your leaders. Either shut up or refrain from needlessly publicizing any defects.

14) DON'T DODGE ISSUES THAT "MUST" BE DEALT WITH. The success of the Black Gangster Disciple Nation depends largely on the "Behind The Scene" plays of folks who never or seldom get recognition or acclaim. Your rights as a member of the Black Gangster Disciple Nation imply many responsibilities. Instead of seeking missions/responsibilities you like. You will accept those however distasteful, which are essential for the good running of the Black Gangster Disciple Nation. Small jobs well done will prepare you for bigger ones! The folks who are chosen for a mission/responsibility whose response is "why me"? Seldom or never get chosen for positions of responsibilities of greater opportunity. "HE WHO IS

VERY FAITHFUL IN A VERY LITTLE, IS FAITHFUL ALSO IN MUCH"!!!

15) ENCOURAGE, DON'T DISCOURAGE. A "Wet Blanket" is defined as, a person or thing that quenches or dampens enthusiasm, pleasure or the likes. Wet blankets are quick to complain about a situation but are slow to do anything about it. They are more interested in fault finding, than fact finding. They are accustomed to speaking of the nation as "THEY" (i.e., Them people), instead of "WE". Anyone in that frame of mind is not needed in or around the Black Gangster Disciple Nation. Be more anxious to improve this powerful nation. Also, concerned with winning cooperation, than winning arguments.

16) BACK UP WORDS WITH ACTION. It has become the complete delusion of this nation to jump to the conclusion that because we have talked about a problem, we have rarely solved it. Discussions are needed to reach mature decisions but resolutions should be translated into performance.

17) KEEP EXPENSES UNDER CONTROL. Many organizations have had to close shop or severely curtail it's activities because of mismanagement of funds. Those who pay dues have a right to a strict accounting of the use of monies. If you take care of finances. The finances will take care of you.

18) WE MUST KEEP LONG RANGE GOALS IN MIND. Many organizations die because they let themselves get caught up in a mass of details and fail to lay long range plans for the future. The "Chairman" intuitively foresaw this and set goals for the Black Gangster Disciple Nation to reach. Unfortunately, our beloved "Chairman" is engaged in a battle for his life. A battle we must all help him win. For against the oppressor alone; you cannot win! In spite of this battle, we are still strong. But lately, in the midst of our crisis. Folks are beginning to ask, "Where are we headed"? "Is the nation fulfilling it's purpose"? "Do new conditions require a new change of directions"? "Do present methods meet current and future needs"? The answer to those questions are yes, and no! Just because the "Chairman" isn't physically present doesn't mean we can't move forward!

19) PERSEVERE AMIDST SHORTCOMINGS AND DIFFICULTIES. If we are working for high goals. Then, they are worth suffering for. Stay in the thick of things until the very end. Expect frustrations and difficulties. You won't be disappointed! Be ready to start and start again. The "Chairman" will bless you if you keep striving to strengthen the nation. Despite, misunderstanding or ingratitudes; Your willingness to keep going will strengthen both you and the "_ALMIGHTY BLACK GANGSTER DISCIPLE NATION_".

LOVE TO YOU ALL!

Memo. 4:

DATE: SEPTEMBER 7, 1987

TO: THE BROTHERS OF THE STRUGGLE

FROM: THE CHAIRMAN AND BOARD OF DIRECTORS

SUBJECT: WORDS OF WISDOM

MY WORD-MY BOND

When someone says, Yes I will, No I won't, I do, yes or no, this person is usually giving his/her word to a particular someone or something. When someone gives their word, they are giving up something of value, something personal or important to them. They are in essence saying, "you can hold me to that or I commit myself to that particular someone or something". A person lives their word to show that they can be trusted.

When a person commits themselves, for example, to a baseball team, job, school, a particular organization or group of people, you are saying you will not default on this. If a person defaults on his word they are usually ashamed, embarrassed or looked down upon.

No responsible individual with self respect will allow upon himself this type of degradation and humiliation. So a person of dignity will be aware, and take the initiative to guard himself and say, "Is my word my bond? Can I be relied upon and trusted?". Do you give you all (100%) to your commitments? If you do, then its because of your dignity and loyalty to yourself and your cause.

Always be sincere when giving your word, be a person to yourself and one that can be relied upon and trusted.

"Always be the type of individual whom people can look upon and say, there goes a person you can count on.".

Make your word, your bond.

Sincerely,

The Chairman and the Board of Directors

Different Names

In his numerous memos to fellow gang members within the prison system and those still outside on the street, Hoover used many names to describe himself and the gang. However, in the end, it was still the same Gangster Disciples or Gangster Disciple Nation.

Brothers of the Struggles

Hoover often used fellow "Brothers in the Struggle" to give the GDs a sense of activism. The idea behind this was to make GDs all believe they were in a struggle for their freedom from the shackles of poverty and political oppression.

Political Prisoners

Since Hoover was sentenced to 150 and more years for ordering the killing of William "Pookey" Young, he took up the position of a political prisoner. At the time of his sentencing, he was the only gang leader that got such harsh treatment, and many believed it was a political move to serve as a deterrent to other fellow street gangs.

Larry often said he was not even the one who pulled the trigger, so he didn't deserve such a long sentence. He started to put himself in the same category as the Nelson Mandela's of this world.

Ghetto Prisoner #1829

"But, Brothers and Sisters, we must have more than strength. We must have vision, too. We must see that we, ourselves, are the victims of the crimes that ignorance, poverty, hopelessness and drugs lead us to commit. We must see that, just as no man is an island, we all wear the shackles of the ghetto. We are all Ghetto Prisoners." Extract from one of Hoover's many memos to the Gangster Disciples.

"Ghetto Prisoner" was another title Hoover used several times to describe himself and fellow GDs incarcerated across the country. According to federal agents, the term "Ghetto Prisoner" was a deliberate dubious attempt to help Hoover gain legitimacy. Another example of Hoover positioning himself as a political prisoner rather than a violent street gang leader. The "Ghetto Prisoner" concept's popularity was relatively strong - there was a new line of designer-gang clothing named after it, along with jerseys of various sports, and the sale price ranged upwards from $45. These items' sales were made through Ghetto Prisoners, Inc, owned and managed by Hoover's common-law wife, Winndye Jenkins, with the company being located in Jenkin's residence.

However, the Ghetto Prisoner company was raided in 1995 by the feds and criminal division of the IRS. Among items seized were company records and $67,000 in cash.

A Season of Shootings, Flipping, and Exodus

After Hoover was sentenced to six life sentences for his role in the sale of narcotics while still in prison, the Gangster Disciples was shaken, and the streets became uncomfortable for them.

First, it was the Feds harassing and arresting anyone who had any form of contact with Hoover while he was in prison. Those arrested were more than 38, while those convicted were around eight at the time. Gang members started snitching on each other to buy their way out of trouble.

Meanwhile, an order to shoot and kill all members who were working with the Feds was activated on the street. Consequently, several informant members or suspected snitcheswere gunned down in a violent manner. While all this was going on, some other members were giving up on the gang. It was too foolish to keep holding onto any form of hope.

One former GD member, Ricky Harris, talked about how Larry Hoover ran the Gangster Disciple chapter from prison.

Ricky (Slick Rick), who had become inactive after the Feds raided the streets searching for gang members after Hoover's arrest, spent his time working at a hardware store installing burglary bars for clients. When he was not installing, he was committing burglary.

In 1995, Ricky was arrested and jailed in the Cook County Prison, and in his court testimony, he talked about his time in prison and how he encountered the GDs. On his first day, he was approached by two men who wanted to know if he was "hooked," and he confirmed to them that he was a Gangster Disciple.

Later that day, a unit coordinator, a top gang leader, came to confirm his references in the guise of delivering toiletries. The leader later confirmed that Ricky was indeed a GD. If he were not in the gang's "good grace," he would have been beaten up mercilessly and taken out on a stretcher to Cermak Hospital.

Immediately after his confirmation, he was loaded and engaged in GD literature, a mandatory requirement. He also learned the "creed," which he recited by heart in court. According to Ricky, "It is a paean to Gangster Disciple Leader, Larry Hoover, which referred to him as Our Honorable Chairman and it further talked about the vision of Our Great Leader."

Gang members were mandated to attend regular meetings to discuss several topics, such as how they were treated in prison, weekly dues, security, and other topics brought up by the Chairman of the Board. Violating these meetings could lead to severe punishment. Ricky cited an example when a riot broke out in prison in 1985, and two GD members tried to escape. That was a violation of the law that required members to "aid and assist." The next day both men were hospitalized after they were beaten up as a form of punishment.

You cannot fight back when you are being beaten; otherwise, it will get worse. You have to accept it as your punishment for a wrongdoing.

All of these were the methods the Gangsters Disciplesadopted to instill discipline amongst its members behind bars. It was also part of the reason they had a formidable bond.

Ricky also elaborated on how the 21st CenturyVOTE was a conduit for drug funds, payment of salary, and phone bills of associates.

Ricky was one of the former gang members who worked with the Federal agents and testified against Larry Hoover. He was a member of GD for almost two decades but came to the court in a wheelchair after falling off while trying to escape what he thought was an assassination attempt on his life. Ricky claimed he saw shadowy figures lurking around his corner, and thought they were coming for him.

Another gang person who flipped on the gang and worked as an informant for the Feds was Charles Banks. Prosecutors played the tape of how he arranged to buy a quantity of cocaine from a GD member. Banks and another police officer, who posed as his cousin, witnessed the transaction.

In what appeared as an obvious hit, 28 year old Banks was shot multiple times in the head while stepping out of his car on the 11,000 Block in South Ashland Avenue. On the list of those who served as witnesses for the State was Bertha Mosby, Larry Hoover's long-time girlfriend.

Word on the street started making the rounds that Larry Hoover was never coming back; that he was never going to be freed. Instead, he would definitely die in prison this time. To many of them, who had thought he was only a few months or years from being released due to his recent popularity and activities in and outside the prison walls, all hope was lost, and they had to move on. It is on record that at this time, several gang members exited the Gangster Disciples for rival gangs like the Vice Lords and Stone Peace Rangers.

Efforts to Free Larry Hoover

Over the years, there have been efforts to get Larry Hoover paroled. Several prominent names have been involved in the effort to get him out of prison. Here is an example of efforts to get Hoover out.

A Copy of the Cover Sheet for the 1995 Petition Drive to Get Larry Hoover a Parole.

"PETITION TO PAROLE LARRY HOOVER

We, the undersigned do hereby acknowledge, agree and thereby join with Prince Asiel Ben Isreal, Co-Chairman, Target Hope--Crime and Violence Committee; Wallace "Gator" Bradley, International Spokesman, United in Peace Organization; Earl King, CEO, and Founder, No Dope Express Foundation; Pat Hogan, Director, Community Affairs, 21st Century V.O.T.E.; Howard Saffold of PACT; Rev. Harold Bailey, Director, and Founder, Probation Challenge; Diana L. Arnold, Proprietor, Absolute Secretarial Services and Graphics Design Layout, Inc; Rev. Helen Sinclair, Ma Houston Prison Outpost; Janette Wilson, Executive Director, Operation PUSH; Margaret Burrells, DuSable Museum; Sid Finley, Executive Director, NAACP (Chicago); Former Mayor Eugene Sawyer; Gary Gardner, President, Soft Sheen Products; Joe Gardner, Commissioner, Metropolitan Water Reclamation

District; Alderman Allan Streeter, 17th Ward; Alderman Shirley Coleman, 16th Ward; Alderman Virgil Jones, 15th Ward; Pastor T.L. Barrett, Jr., Founder, Life Center Church of Universal Awareness; Hal Baskin, Executive Director, P.E.A.C.E. Organization; and Virgil Martin, Honor Student, Fenger High School.

We hereby, individually and collectively, do believe, as evidence of his present actions, Larry Hoover, to be rehabilitated and of sound mind and judgment, and as such, an asset to the communities-at-large in the capacity of a prime component in the institution, maintenance and subsequent longevity of the existing United in Peace Coalition Nations' Truce that currently attributes to the continuous, dramatic drop in the percentage of violent crimes and homicides in the African-American communities from Chicago to Peoria and throughout the State of Illinois.

We hereby, individually and collectively, do ask Governor Jim Edgar and the Illinois Prisoner Review Board and its Chairman to grant Larry Hoover parole."

There were many more of these types of efforts and support to get the Chairman of the Board out of prison. However, law enforcement officers believe that the streets will worsen if Hoover is released back into society. They claim that Hoover has not shown signs of being rehabilitated.

Investigations would later reveal that several of the petitioners were on the Gangster Disciple's payroll. Some were said to have received as much as $50,000 to appear or put their names on the parole appeal. Another good example is the case of one Alderman, Allan Streeter, who wrote several letters using official government letterheads seeking Hoover's release. Below is one of those letters.

June 15, 1993

Mr. James Williams, Chairman

Illinois Prisoner Review Board

319 East Madison

Springfield, IL 62701

Re: Larry Hoover, C01829, Vienna Correctional Center

Dear Mr. Williams:

I am writing to you as a concerned citizen to support the release of Mr. Larry Hoover who has demonstrated a sincere desire and effort in working for the improvement of the African American Community.

For example, Mr. Hoover was one of the first to sign the Peace Treaty to stop the killings in the African American Community, which has been very successful. Also, Mr. Hoover has been very instrumental in working for the capture of the Chatham Community Rapist and working to assist in the apprehension of a serial killer in the Chatham area.

I strongly urge you, as Chairman of the Illinois Prisoner Review Board, to use your legal and executive powers to work for the release of this servant of the community.

Thank you in advance for your consideration and prompt attention to this matter.

Sincerely,

(signed)

Allan Streeter

Alderman, 17th Ward

The alderman was later convicted for corrupt practices during Operation Silver Shovel.

In what seems like one of the most audacious efforts yet to get Hoover out of prison, celebrity rapper, Kanye West, who is from the same Chicago area as Larry Hoover, visited Donald Trump in the

Whitehouse and asked the President to free Larry Hoover. Here's what West had to say about Larry Hoover's situation.

"because he started doing positive for the community. He started showing that he actually had power. That he wasn't just one of a monolithic voice, that could wrap people around."

"There's infinite amounts of the universe and there's alternate universe," he said. *"So it's very important for me to get Hoover out because in an alternate universe, I am him and I have to go and get him free. Because he was doing positive inside Chicago just like I'm moving back to Chicago, and it's not just about, you know, getting on stage and being an entertainer and having a monolithic voice that's forced to be a specific part."*

Again, there was high hope that the former President would pardon Hoover before leaving office, but it never happened.

However, all hope is not lost, at least not on the streets. There are several people still agitating for the freedom of Larry Hoover, especially through Drill music. These young dudes see him as a charismatic figure who is suffering for them all. Youtube and all the platforms are littered with songs about King Larry Hoover, the Chairman of the Board. There are shirts and other souvenirs with the inscription "Free Larry Hoover".

However, the voices clamoring for the freedom of Hoover are not as strong as they were before the federal indictments. These divides can be clearly seen on the streets among the gangs. Unlike when David Barksdale and Larry Hoover ran the street under one name, the Black Gangster Disciple Nation, what followed after Hoover's arrest was more than just a breakaway or a breakup. It was a total breakdown of order and vicious rivalry between the Black Disciples loyal to David Barksdale and the Gangster Disciples devoted to Larry Hoover.

Let's take a deep look into these two former alliances, now arch-rivals.

Chapter Four

The Structure of the Black Disciples

The Growth of the Black Disciples

When Hoover and his Gangster Disciples fell out of favor, and the former was sent to 6 consecutive life sentences following a federal investigation, the Black Disciples were the biggest gainers of that time. GD gang members flipped and switched alliances with ease. Before this time, there was no need to switch alliances because the GDs and BDs were allies against other rival gangs like the Black P. Stones, Mickey Cobras, and Vice Lords. But now that the GDs were in troubled waters, snitching and shooting its members, the BD was a natural alternative.

A silent war between the Gangster Disciples and the Black Disciples over who controlled what drug territory soon degenerated into a permanent street war. When this happened, swing GDs could flip to BD and sever all ties with GD. Gradually, the Black Disciples started gaining prominence and recognition on the street and with law enforcement.

In January 1996, a Gangster Disciple Governor, Chuck Dorsey, aka "Big Chuck," was shot and killed on the streets. The BDs and GDs had a meeting on 38th and Cottage Grove in the Bronze Ville area following his death. Both gangs were allies at 38th and Ellis and around the Ida B. Wells and Madden Park project vicinities. Chuck's death was expected to lead to an all-out street war in these areas and the "Low End" at 46th and Evans 5th Ward Boulevard. In fact, at the meeting, Rimrod threw down the pitchfork as a sign of disrespect to the GDs, but still, there was no violence. Many would attribute this non-violent approach to the recent weakness and depletion rocking the Gangster Disciple.

So, instead of violence over the death of their governor, GD lost more members, which led to the BDs having more members on the Low End and in the Projects. A few days after the peace meeting, Rimrod, who disrespected the GDs at the meeting, was gunned down and killed, along with some high-ranking Black Disciples.

Among the recruits who joined BD at this period was Robert Sandifer, aka "Yummy," an 11-year-old boy. Yummy was a troubled kid who was notorious for stealing cars and breaking into houses since he was 8-years-old. He had been known to law enforcement since he was only three years old.

The 90s and 2000s belonged to the Black Disciples as they grew in numbers and notoriety. They also climbed to the top 10 largest gangs in Chicago, with members in different suburbs across the United States. All the while, an outright turf war had broken out between the GDs and the Black Disciples. It was like a case of, "if you snooze, you die." Violent gunfire erupted in the Robert Taylor and Stateway Gardens projects, with bullets flying back and forth day and night in several exchanges between the two rival gangs. These two gangs claimed control over the public housing complexes, with other gangs having no say. The BDs eventually overcame the Gangster Disciples through higher numbers and more substantial firepower. These boosted their reputation on the streets, and more teenagers saw them as the more powerful and best gang to join.

In 1991, the Black Disciples moved their operations a notch higher when they took over the 16 story Randolph Tower housing authority complex in the Washington Park neighborhood at 6217 S. Calumet Avenue. This structure was named "The Castle." They fortified the structure and set up a complex narcotic business that authorities believe was doing from $45,000 to $300,000 daily in crack cocaine and heroin. Marvel Thompson managed the structure, and all visitors were searched before entering and exiting at the door by armed gang members with automatic rifles. The Castle became a place of refuge for the BD and their operations. According to law enforcement, part of the funds generated from the drug activities in the Tower went into money laundering, investment in clubs like the Atlanta Nightclub, real estate, and even bankrolling rap artists like the MOB, among many others.

Snippers with night vision goggles were strategically located at the top of the building and other locations to ensure their operations' safety. The Castle was not a friendly place for the Chicago Police Department, especially after one undercover officer was shot. The officer survived because he was wearing a bulletproof vest.

The Black Disciples keep pushing their luck and showing off their power and influence. They hijacked the WCFL 104.7 radio owned by a Christian radio station in the Morris suburb. They featured various music on this frequency to the surprise of several listeners. It was also believed that the frequency served as a communication link with The Castle to alert them of any threats from law enforcement or rival street gangs, like the Gangster Disciples.

However, in 2004, the Chicago Police carried out an operation that led to the raiding of the Tower, and the arrest of several gang members. City authorities would later decide that the best way to check and curb the operations of the gang was to tear down the tower. Later that year, the building known as the HQ of the BDs, named the "The Castle," was finally razed to the ground. The structure was the single most extensive location where the Black Disciples had ever run its operations. However, after being displaced for some time, they regrouped and continued to grow their operations and membership.

While the authorities were busy taking down the Robert Taylor buildings, the Black Disciples expanded into new territories like 43rd down to 49th and State. The gang also took over the 5th Ward and New Town before the Tower was wholly taken down in 2006. The gang expanded its operations and opened up in the Burnside area, South Deering, Riverdale, Washington, Pullman, West Pullman,

Morgan Park, and Washington Heights neighborhoods. Their expansion continued into several cities in the United States. What started as a rival street gang has since grown into a complex organization.

The Organizational Structure

Most of the Chicago street gangs are made up of young boys and girls who had very little to do with schooling, not to mention acquiring any formal knowledge of running a proper organization. From the leadership to the foot soldiers, these young guys depend on their street smarts, guns, and the survival nature of the slums to run the gang's affairs.

Known leaders like Larry Hoover of the Gangster Disciples and David Barksdale of Black Disciples had little to zero education when they formed these gangs. However, they developed street gangs into organizations running complex operations, which have outlived most of the founders. While Gangster Disciples ran their operations like a corporate business, the Black Disciples, on the other hand, was structured like a religious gang with their leaders called "Ministers."

The BDs have several "sets" across Chicago and the US. Each set is made of 30 to 40 members, and they are called "dynasties." Each dynasty is structured similarly to the main body, with the same organizational structure.

Each dynasty runs a simple organogram in the following order;

- King David. Even in death, every gang member still reveres him.
- Next is King Shorty - Jerome Freeman, also known as the "The Crowned King."
- One level below the Crowned King are Ministers.
- After that, we have the Assistant Co-Ministers.
- Next is the First Demetrius.

- The lowest-ranked members are called Soldiers or Representatives.

In each dynasty, there are a few temporary positions right below the First Demetrius;

- Chief of Violations.
- Chief of Security.
- Assistant Chief of Security.

These roles are often rotated because they have unrewarded responsibilities. The work that goes into the above three far outweighs the financial benefits sothey are rotated among the members chosen by the First Demetrius.

As it is called in the Black Disciples, the dynasty is similar in operation to what is obtainable in the Gangster Disciples; they are the middle management team and the heart of the operations. Other positions come up sometimes, like "dons" and generals, and each also has its deputies. Most of the sales and money pass through the middle management class up to the dynasty leaders, then to the higher leadership of the gang's hierarchy.

Every dynasty is headed by a Minister who is typically 25 years and older. His role is to supervise and assign responsibilities to the Assistant Co-Cinister and the First Demetrius. The Assistant Co-minister is responsible for facilitating the sales of narcotics and other businesses. He is also responsible for collecting dues from members of his set.

The First Demetrius' role is to keep an eye on every gang member in his chapter. He also calls meetings, distributes gang literature, and ensures each member stays on course while working for the gang. Part of the requirements for qualifying for the positions of Assistant Co-Minister and First Demetrius is that members have to be 18 years and above.

The Primary Business

Many people, especially non-insiders, assume these street gangs exist basically to wage war against each other, and when they are not doing that, they are probably doing and selling drugs. While that is true, there's more. These gangs hold meetings where they iron out issues affecting the gangs and other rivals. They also hold parties and picnics. Top on the list of the agendas for these meetings is reaching more localities and taking out their rivals, among others. It's also an avenue to dish out punishment to errant members.

Like the Gangster Disciples and other rival gangs, the Black Disciples have a unique handshake, gang logos, and written and unwritten codes. However, the BD is littered with teenage boys and girls who delight in illegal activities like their rivals. Their primary role is to trade in drugs. These are primarily underage kids who have already been exposed to the other side of life. Most of them have not known any other life than being on the street among gang members. Going to jail for these young kids is like getting a medal of honor.

The term "Putting in Nation's Work" is commonly used among the BDs, and it simply means selling drugs for the dynasty. Another common phrase is "Getting New Work," which means collecting a new batch of drugs for sale. This could mean picking up ten bags of marijuana. After the sale of this batch, the individual returns the proceeds for the sale of seven out of the ten batches to the Minister and keeps the balance from the sale of the other three for themself as profit.

Again, like the GDs, the majority of the operations for the BDs are centered around drug sales, and the proceeds go from the bottom to the top of the hierarchy. However, strict rules have been put in place to shield the gang leadership from criminal prosecutions.

In addition to the BDs' drug dealings were a gambling enterprise. For the most part, the setting was an apartment in a public housing complex, a house used for drug operations, an open deserted space, or a member's house. The gambling was in the form of large-scale crap games.

This gambling also occured during the gang's annual picnic, which is on the 24th and 25th of May. It was later revealed that the BDs were involved in gambling all over and on everything from the Superbowl to fights and just about anything they could place a bet on. However, the dice and large crap games are their all-time favorites. Sometimes they have up to 30 to 40 people betting on these games with stringent security to ensure the players and the watchers are not interrupted. These betting fees range from a couple of dollars to hundreds and thousands per bet. At these games, everything you can think of is available, including drugs, automatic weapons, and fights.

The Black Disciples also have several safe houses to carry on their business, including sales and distribution of drugs, packaging, and gambling. They try to soundproof all their safe houses to lock in the noise, especially the sound of a gunshot. These soundproof buildings are also needed for their dog-fight gambling activities. These dog fights are usually fought to the death by one of the dogs. During the pre-show stage of the main dog fight event, you would see a handler throw in a cat to get a reaction from the dogs and the crowd. The cats are often devoured by the stern-looking, vicious dogs.

Upholding Internal Discipline

Like legally registered bodies like not-for-profit organizations, churches, and other bodies, the Black Disciples have rules and regulations that govern the gang's activities. These rules are known and are expected to be followed by each gang member. These rules focus on keeping the group's unity while ensuring the smooth operations of their drug operations across the cities. Check out some internal documents at the end of this chapter.

Violating the rules that govern the group's operation would attract public punishment in the presence of other group members to serve as a deterrent to others. Depending on the level or size of the offense, the punishment was usually administered at the general meeting. At the same time, minor violations were handled at the set levels. For example, a minor violation could attract what was called a thirty-second violation. That means that the violator would be held down with his hands tied to his back while other gang members beat and assaulted him for a duration of thirty seconds. Minor violations are in the categories of failure to attend meetings and default on membership dues.

On the other hand, more considerable violations can attract five minutes of beating and assault to death. Like the Gangster Disciples, the Black Disciples have a reputation for killing their members. The massive violations that attract this stiffer punishment are actions that affect the overall gang, like failure to do "nation work." For example, when members steal from the group or fail to return the 70% share belonging to the group from the sales of drugs. Also, when a member loses the stash in their custody. It is also a significant violation for any member to disrespect any BD leader like the Ministers, Assistant Co-ministers, First Demetrius, and others.

Fostering Unity Through House Parties

House parties are a frequent event for the gang members, and anyone can attend these parties for a small, $3 admittance fee. There are no age or gender restrictions, as long as you can pay the admittance fees. The purpose of these parties ranges from showing a unified party to showing social status in the gang and establishing a social status pecking order. High-ranking members are identified and accorded their proper respect as they stand out in the seating arrangements. After gang members have taken their positions, the non-members are offered what is left.

Furthermore, these parties serve as opportunities to recruit new members while attracting members from other gangs to switch sides. House parties are a time for relaxing and bonding, smoking, and taking in drugs without the fear of being busted. It is a time to feel good and gamble with brothers; it is one of those moments when your membership counts for something a little more. These house parties are mostly where issues of violations like disrespecting senior members happen, especially under the influence of alcohol and drugs. Members are primarily careful in the jokes and comments about other gang members, especially the "bosses." You cannot even express how you detest a fellow member because you would be violating the gang's rules.

House parties also serve as opportunities to honor the birthday of Black Disciple leaders in that area. They are presented with cakes designed with the symbol of the gang to honor them as leaders and to hold down that area. Leaders also use the opportunities to take photos (mostly polaroids). These cakes usually carry the six-point star of David, and inside the star will be the symbol "III," which is the symbol of the Black Disciple gang. At the top of the star, you will have the word "King," and right at the bottom, another word, "David," will be designed. To the left of the cake will be the names of other top gang leaders dead and alive, including the ones in that area and, of course, the celebrant.

Meeting and Venues

The BDs use different locations for the venues of their meetings. The choice of location also depends on the nature of the meeting. If the weather is good and warm, a large back porch will work as a meeting point. Otherwise, an enclosed large garage or an abandoned building will be just fine.

Violations and due defaulting are the predominant issues on the agendas at these meetings. Dues which are $5, are also collected at the meetings. The frequencies of these meetings are at the discretion of the Ministers, but on average, two meetings are held in a dynasty per month, and each time a meeting is called, members are expected to come with a $5 due.

Attending meetings for the BDs is an entirely different ball game. It is a time of fear and panic because you never know why the meeting was called and what will go down at the meeting. One common fear among the BDs is the fear of being ratted out by another member. For example, when a meeting is in session, you may be singled out to recite the group's prayer, anthem, or any part of the gang's literature at random. Failure to recite any of the gang's famous slogans will be deemed as a violation because you are expected to know the gang's literature like the back of your hand. These slogans are sacred to the BD as a whole, and every member is expected to know them and be ready to recite them when called upon. It is as vital as the air they breathe.

Female Members

Female involvement is allowed in the Black Disciples. However, it fits the chivalry hypothesis, where the "sister," as they are called, are treated with more leniency than their male counterparts. The Chicago street gangs are primarily male-dominated, authoritarian, cult-like institutions where ladies have very little chance of rising to the helm of affairs, even in dynasties where the sisters constitute up to 30% of the membership. On paper, the BD seems to be open to female leadership, but in reality, no female has ever risen to any position of reputation in the long history of the gang. This could also be because the ladies are not "sexed in" as an initiation ceremony, which may result from the fact that most of the chapters are based on small neighborhoods, covering merely a block or "turf."

However, there's a separate wing reserved for hardcore female gang members in the membership plan. They are known as the "Daughters of the Universal Star." This is a rare all-female chapter of the gang. They hold their meetings and appoint leaders, and like their male counterparts, they command respect and make their own decisions. Make no mistakes; these ladies are as vicious and bloodthirsty as they come. They administer punishments to violators; they sell drugs, they engage in everything the men do. Ultimately, though, there's a cap on how far they can rise in the Black Disciple gang.

Birthday - The Picnics

David Barksdale is still a godly figure to the Black Disciples, and they honor him every time they get the chance to do so. His birthday is one of the most important annual events on the BDs calendar. It's the gang's picnic. Every year on May 24th and 25th, King David's birthday is celebrated with a massive picnic at Ogden Park at 63rd and Racine, a public park on the South Side of Chicago. At the same time, various parties are going on in different locations, all in commemoration of the King's Birthday. It has always been a massive event in the city of Chicago as a whole. You will have several souvenirs like T-shirts, and jerseys with massive images of David Barksdale on the front and back worn by members. The cheapest shirts sell for $50.

Like many gangs, these picnics are held in public places. They are usually massively attended but with stringent rules that members must follow, like, no alcohol, drugs, guns, fighting, and anything illegal. This is also because there are times when politicians and religious leaders in the city have been invited to be part of these picnics. So, these picnics are deliberately made to look like real, wholesome fun.

In 1995, the Black Disciples held a picnic outside Chicago like its rival, the Gangster Disciples. It was in the State of Minnesota. Hundreds of members were transported in large buses across states, especially from Chicago, to attend the picnic. The difference this time around was that members were a little more relaxed than usual. In addition to the assorted food available, members could and did drugs as much as they wanted. Gambling was going on at almost every corner of the gathering. The gang members felt more expressive in the state of Minnesota. So, while the GD focused more on impressing the politicians at their picnics, the Black Disciples liked to express themselves more and focus on King David Barksdale.

Recruitment and Initiations

The BD has developed several attractive ways of wooing new members to join them. In addition to inviting these young guys to various wild parties, they also developed a drug sales strategy that leaves the new member with some pocket money after the sales. They offer these kids a commission-like arrangement where they get cuts from the sales of drugs. It's a massive motivation for kids in these poor neighborhoods; it also offers the opportunity to have a "good time."

At parties, kids are free to live their fantasies of belonging to a gang that protects them, being in a brotherhood, and having a family where they are not judged but looked out for and protected. A closer review of the gang's internal literature revealed that its targets are underage kids and teenagers in their early years.

When they join the gang, they see the body as their religion and the local gang leader as their Minister, and these boys give the top leaders God-like treatment. Part of their orientation is to be ready to kill and die for their leaders and the group at large. These young lads are taken through regular "prayers" with other gang members. These are not just some ordinary prayers as revealed by some internal documents, but a prayer of submission that places a cult-like hold on these kids and makes them have the confidence to shoot in response to the order of their leaders.

The initiation process for recruits is not as dramatic as what is obtainable in other cult-like groups. It's actually relatively straightforward. New members do not have to engage in criminal activities, nor do they have to be beaten or physically assaulted to show how much pain they can withstand. The recruits simply recite the "Trey" on the gang's prayer, and then senior members present will put a "trey" on the heads of the inductees. "Trey on the head" is used to describe the senior members blessing the recruits. They use their three-finger to touch the new guys on their foreheads to welcome them to the gang.

After this exercise, they become gang members and start paying dues while doing their "Nation Work." Just as in other gangs, the bulk of the new members are kids. Hence, they need to do the "Nation Work," which is selling drugs on behalf of the gang for about six years before they become eligible to hold a solid position in the gang. The reality is a large percentage of these kids don't live that long before they are gunned down or arrested and sent to jail. Going to jail or dying in the process of doing the "Nation Work" is seen as a thing of honor and great sacrifice for the good of the gang.

The Black Disciples, like other gangs, provide loads of benefits for members who are in prison serving time. They send money to members in jail for cosmetics and other needs. Books and other relevant items are not in short supply. The only exception is if you were not true to the gang. Members who hold relevant positions still get to keep their positions while being incarcerated.

Prayers, Commitment, and Pledges

The GDs and BDs share common types of literature and prayers. We have put together some of these prayers obtained by the National Gang Crime Research Center. There has not been any correction of grammar or spelling from our end.

Note #1: Prayer said in reverence of the late David Barksdale

PRAYER

Let us open up this prayer with a lot of love to KING of all Kings, KING DAVID, our crowned KING, KING SHORTY, and all righteous Black Disciples of the world...

We are stronger together, we are stronger together, my love and yours forever. We are as ONE.

King David said that is must be done! God put the stars in the sky, and with the reflection they shine.

Yes said King David, we must combine, Body, Souls, and Minds, with the D's Love for now and all times.

Note #2: A Prayer of Love

*ALMIGHTY BLACK DISCIPLE NATION * * * * * **

Once the D's thang was just an idea until KING DAVID said it's time to bring it here. Just like everything else it had to begin, but the BLACK DISCIPLE NATION will never end.

Love, Life, and Loyalty will get it all started but without WISDOM, KNOWLEDGE, and UNDERSTANDING it will soon be departed.

The SIX POINTED STAR will connect them all together, since it is the STAR OF KING DAVID that will make it all last forever.

Being able to use 360 degrees of pure knowledge in any situation means nothing is impossible for the BLACK DISCIPLE NATION.

*By using the knowledge of the SIX POINTED STAR means we can better our situation no matter where we are, whether behind these walls, out there on the streets doing our own thang the BLACK DISCIPLE NATION shall remain the same. Let us give thanks. I AM WHAT I AM, A BLACK DISCIPLE, AND THAT I AIN'T I WILL NEVER BE * * * * * **

We are going to close this prayer with a lot of love to KING of all Kings, KING DAVID, our CROWNED KING, KING SHORTY, AND ALL RIGHTEOUS BLACK DISCIPLES OF THE WORLD.

Note #3: The Universal Code of Law that governs the activities all members - 1st Part

ALMIGHTY BLACK DISCIPLE NATION

UNIVERSAL CODE OF LAWS

PART I

1. I solemnly swear to never disrespect the KING or "any" member of the Black Disciple Nation.

2. I will not tolerate anyone scandalizing the name of the Black Disciple Nation.

3. I will sacrifice my life for the Nation's causes.

4. I will Love, Respect, and Honor every member of the nation as I so love, respect, and honor myself.

5. I will be of any assistance to any member of the Nation in any problems or difficulties that he have, be it physically or mentally.

6. I will accept no other teachings than that of our KING or that which refers to the Nation.

7. I will not tolerate anyone, even a Black Disciple to misrepresent or disrespect our appraisal emblem or flag.

8. I pledge my soul, heart, love and spirit to the Black Disciple nation and will be a part of it even in death.

9. I will not affiliate myself with our opposition.

10. I will abide by all commands given to me by the KING and all appointed chiefs.

11. I will not tolerate the criticizing or abusive sayings of those who are not Black Disciple.

12. I will not tolerate anyone criticizing the KING or any righteous member of the Black Disciple Nation.

13. I will ask and accept the same penalty that any Black Disciple is given for my transgression against the Nation's Laws.

14. I will not fight or mistreat any Nation member unless told to do so otherwise.

15. I will not fight against any member of the Black Disciple Nation and will not stand to see any member of the Black Disciple Nation fight among themselves.

16. I will greet and salute any member of the Black Disciple Nation with the crossing of the CLENCHED FIST, the warriors sign whenever and where ever I see any Black Disciple.

Note #4. The Universal Code of Law that governs the activities all members - 2nd Part

ALMIGHTY BLACK DISCIPLE NATION

UNIVERSAL CODE OF LAWS PART II

1. All soldiers must share and respect a code of silence, loyalty to friends inside the nation, also becomes a part of that code and the two (silence and loyalty) join to establish the soldiers as insiders and everyone else as outsiders.

2. Family disrespect cannot and will not be tolerated either toward each other or family members of his fellow soldiers.

3. No soldier shall encourage the use of drugs to any soldier or family members of his fellow soldiers.

4. No soldier shall consume any addictive drugs.

5. No soldier shall encourage prostitution from the women in their families or families of fellow soldiers.

6. No soldier shall point out, refer or introduce any fellow member to an outsider without first screening and checking into the background of that outside person.

7. At no time shall a soldier shall point out, refer, or introduce any outsider to the "King", or any of the places the "King" might be without permission from the proper chain of Command.

8. No soldier shall bring inside the nation new members without a screening and an observation period and the approval of an evaluation report by the top of the chain of command.

9. All soldiers regardless of rank or position must strive to help each other and not compete with each other.

Note #5: This Literature explains the symbols of the Black Disciple

MAY THE STAR OF DAVID WATCH OVER US ALL AS DISCIPLES

BLACK DISCIPLES NATION THIS EMBLEM STANDS AS FLAG

FOR THE BLACK DISCIPLE NATION

1. The HEART represents the LOVE we have for our Nation.

2. The CROWN represents our Nation's Crowned King, KING SHORTY.

3. The SIX POINTED STAR of KING DAVID represents what our Nation is based on.

4. The SWORD represents Life and Death in our Nation, Life and the survival of the Nation at all cost. But Death before Dishonor.

5. The DEVIL'S PITCHFORK represents our Nation's powers and our struggle to overcome the oppression we are under.

6. The HORNS represent our Nation's determination to overcome all obstacles.

7. The DEVIL'S TAIL represents the oppression that Blacks, Latinos, and Third World people live under and is not a white issue.

8. The FLAME represents our Nation's eternal philosophy of Self-Help.

9. The Insignia "78" represents the year of our Nation's New Day of Teachings and Inspiration.

Note #6:

THE SIX POINTED STAR AND OUR COLORS

The STAR OF KING DAVID is our Nation's symbol. It has six points, and each point of the star stands for: LOVE, LIVE, LOYALTY, UNITY, KNOWLEDGE, and UNDERSTANDING.

The Disciple's colors are: RED, BLACK, and BLUE. Red is for the bloodshed of our Nation. Black stands for all black people. Blue is for the heavenly sky which blesses all Disciples. True blue also represents the love we share, which is as deep as the deep blue sea.

Note #7: Star of David

THE SIX POINTS AND THEIR MEANINGS

1. LOVE: Love of the Nation is greater than mere love alone, because we have a brotherhood in which love is as deep as the deep blue sea. TRUE BLUE LOVE.

2. LIFE: Life commitment to the Nation for the betterment of ourselves as well as the Nation and each committed brother within the Nation, and our Nation's teachings, laws, creeds, symbols, philosophy and defense.

3. LOYALTY: To yourself, and each committed brother of our Nation.

4. UNITY: Collectively embrace all concepts, ideas, and actions that apply to our Nation. Togetherness is essential in order for us to continue our survival.

5. KNOWLEDGE: Is insight, therefore it is priceless, it gives one the ability to apply rational judgment. Knowledge is the ability to have a conscious awareness, and knowledge gained and not passed along is wasted knowledge.

6. UNDERSTANDING: Shows that we are able to communicate effectively, bring about agreements, and a positive state of mind.

"Repeat these six points (PRINCIPLES) until they are fully understood, because they apply to you (ALL) as BLACK DISCIPLES. KING SHORTY IS KING! AND LONG LIVE THE KING.

BD. LOYALTY

Note #8: The Ten Commandments

ALMIGHTY BLACK DISCIPLE NATION'S TEN COMMANDMENTS

1. Thou shall love the nation with all thy heart, soul and spirit.

2. Thou shall teach the warriors of thy nation diligently and shall talk with, advise, and in the event that some go astray, thou shall be there to understand and restore in them the determination of a true Disciple.

3. Thou shall bind them together in UNITY and LOVE, and they shall be as true as one that will never be divided.

4. Thou shall make it known in the streets, jails and penitentiaries that this Black Disciple Nation is indestructible.

5. It shall be that when we have fully accepted the teachings of our deceased KING DAVID and our CROWNED KING, KING SHORTY, then, and only then, shall we acquire the riches that are rightfully ours as Disciples in the armor of blue.

6. For the nation is full of good things that thou has brought us into, therefore, we can never fail but shall prosper at all cost.

7. Beware lest we forget the teachings of the King that brought us into awareness of this Black Disciple Nation.

8. Thou shall feel the warmth of this Black Disciple Nation and serve the King and swear by the power of his name which he has invested in the Nation.

9. You shall not seek the safety of other nations around you, but hold steadfast to the teachings of the Black Disciple Nation.

10. For the King is a jealous King, he loves his people, and unless we return this love as it is freely given, we shall anger the King, and thus bring forth upon ourselves the wrath of the Black Disciple Nation.

Note #9: Commitment and loyalty

A DAILY REMINDER

WHAT IT MEAN TO TRULY BE A DISCIPLE

I AM WHAT I AM, A BLACK DISCIPLE, AND THAT I AIN'T WILL NEVER BE * * * * * *

1. As a true Disciple I am a follower of thy Crowned King, KING SHORTY, and a student in the teachings of our nation's Founder and King of all Kings, KING DAVID.

2. I shall strive and succeed in showing myself to be disciplined in my actions, and thoughts, reflecting to the fullest of my ability and potential the SIX PRINCIPLES WITHIN THE STAR OF DAVID.

3. I shall seek to be mindful of the TEN COMMANDMENTS of our nation and the UNIVERSAL CODES OF LAW.

4. I shall do whatever is possible, or whatever is asked and required of me, to support the leadership of our organization.

5. I shall especially be conscious of my environment, its elements and dangers therein, and shall secure myself and each righteous member of our organization from the dangers and pitfalls before us.

6. I shall remind myself and my brothers that * * * * * * WE ARE STRONGER TOGETHER, WE ARE STRONGER TOGETHER, MY LOVE AND YOURS FOREVER. WE ARE AS ONE. KING DAVID SAID THAT IT MUST BE DONE! GOD PUT THE STARS IN THE SKY, AND WITH THE REFLECTION THEY SHINE. YES SAID KING DAVID WE MUST COMBINE, BODY, SOULS, AND MINDS, WITH THE D'S LOVE FOR NOW AND ALL TIMES.

I vow this day to shine . . .

For a gang led by predominantly unschooled kids, it has quite a lot of literature, and all members are expected to recite these prayers and commandments by heart.

Chapter Five

The Story of Robert (Yummy) Sandifer

As mentioned earlier, the Black Disciples, like the Gangster Disciples and many street gangs, kill their own members. In 1994, like their street arch-rivals, it was the turn of the BDs to gain local, national, and international attention when it ordered the killing of another member, an 11-year-old child. The murder rocked the gang and shook it to its foundation. It was so bad that TIME Magazine featured the story on its front page twice that year. Let's look into this story and find out what happened.

It was supposed to be a typical day in the Chicago South Side, a bright day where everyone went about their regular business, except it wasn't. It was another sad day and just a fortnight apart. Parents in the neighborhood brought out their children to attend a dead boy's vigil. The boy was known to many and unknown to others.

Some parents wanted their kids to be part of the event and watch as the boy lay in the coffin, cold and lifeless to serve as a warning to them about their life choices. For other parents, it was one death too many in the neighborhood. They recalled how the tears from losing a 14-year-old girl had barely dried from their faces, and now they were here again to bury an 11-year-old. Yet other parents saw the whole thing as Karma because of how related the two deaths were.

They lined up to watch the young boy's lifeless body lying in the coffin, almost as if he were asleep. Parents made their kids take a peek into the coffin, and they saw the stitches that covered the point where bullets were fired through the back of his head. The picture for the funeral did not go unnoticed. It was a mugshot, and it seemed that was the only picture his parents could provide. That said a lot. These images will haunt parents, their kids, and the whole community for a long time to come.

Laying lifeless in the coffin was 11-year-old Robert Sandifer, popularly known as "Yummy" by many. He was a Black Disciples street gang member. Many at the vigil had different opinions about the boy, how he lived his life and his eventual death. Yummy got his nickname from his love for junk food, especially cookies when he was a little boy. According to a local shop owner, Yummy was a "son of a bitch" who he had banned from his store because he was always coming there to steal from him. He explained how Yummy was always in trouble and outmuscling other kids and concluded that no one would be sorry to see him gone.

It seems as though everyone had been expecting this kid's death because it was barely a fortnight before this time that they lost Shavon Dean to stray bullets from Yummy's gun. Yummy, who was out on a mission from his Black Disciple gang to shoot down some members of the Gangster Disciples, ended up wounding them. At the same time, a stray bullet from his gun hit Shavon Dean, and she died on the spot. The police started combing the neighborhood for the killer of Shavon as the news filled the air and brought unwanted attention to the gang and its activities. The Black Disciples helped Yummy and covered up for him for a few days but later felt the heat was too much and feared Yummy might crack if arrested. So, they ordered for him to be killed. That was how he became a victim, within 14 days of his victim. His lifeless, bloody body was found in a mud puddle under a railway viaduct three days after being shot. His death disturbed the whole city.

Early Childhood and Education

The Mayor of Chicago at that time commented about the killing of Yummy and how it related to Shavon Dean's death, saying Yummy was one of the boys who had slipped through the cracks. He was right. Yummy was no stranger to the authorities; they knew him for almost all of his short lifetime. His mother was a teenage addict while his father was languishing in jail. As a toddler, Yummy was beaten, and as a student, he was away from school for more days than he attended. The child shuttled between detention houses that could not keep him detained, homes, and gang safe houses. He was a known face with the police authorities due to multiple arrests. Still, there was little they could do because he was only a child and the Illinois laws prevented them from putting him on probation. Also, thirteen local juvenile homes could not admit him because he was just a child.

Yummy had always been a very mean, walking weapon that found solace amid a gang that took advantage of him. The crimes he committed and the one he eventually suffered shook the nation's heart more than the whole history of gangster life in Chicago and every street in the country. *"If ever there was a case where the kid's future was predictable, it was this case. What you've got here is a kid who was made and turned into a sociopath by the time he was three years old."* said Cook County public guardian Patrick Murphy. According to his mother, Lorina, Yummy was an average 11-year-old kid. The psychologist, county court judge, and police officer seemed to believe Yummy was a sociopath. *"I see a lot of Roberts,"* said Cook County Circuit Judge Thomas Sumner, who handled charges against Yummy for armed robbery and car theft. *"We see this 100 times a week,"* added Murphy.

The evidence and proof stared everyone in the face when it came to Yummy. He had a file everywhere. His rap sheet was glaring and overwhelming to the public guardian office, the courts, the police, and finally, the medical examiner's office. However, there was nothing different about his file; it was only one of the hundreds and thousands of other African-American kids living in the projects. So, it appears everyone missed noticing that Yummy was not an average child. They all ignored that his brain might have been flooded, which caused him to drown.

Psychological Evaluation

According to the conclusion of a psychiatrist who evaluated Yummy in November 1993, *"Robert is emotionally flooded. His response to the flooding is to back away from demanding situations and act out impulsively and unpredictably."* When asked to complete a sentence that starts with "I am very…." Yummy's response was "Sick." The psychiatrist concluded that Yummy was filled with self-hate, loneliness, uneducated, and wary. He jumped and took cover at the sound of a walkie-talkie along the hallways and claimed the psychiatrist was trying to trick him. Yummy was like most kids from the hood, but his case was a little unique, and it was unclear if anyone would be able to reach out and save him.

Robert's Mother and Abuses

Lorina had Yummy when she was barely 15 years old as her four fathers' third out of ten children. Before him was Lorenzo, then Victor, and others. She never knew her father, dropped out of 10th grade, found a place to live, and survived on welfare while nursing a crack habit all along. She explained to a social worker that she tried to live with the boy's father, but he had a fit of bad anger and was very hot-tempered, so they split. He was later convicted of drug charges and illegal possession of firearms. Lorina was no stranger to law enforcement. In 1984, she was charged with "Child Neglect" when she refused to follow the doctor's instruction to treat her 2-year-old eye condition. Victor, the boy in question, would later go blind. Yummy was brought to the Jackson Park Hospital soaked in blood from scratches and bruises one year later. Barely a month later, it was his sister's turn; her case was a second and third-degree burn on her genitals. Lorina's story was that the girl had fallen on a radiator. The emergency dismissed that claim nurse, who informed the court that the injuries did not match Lorina's story. The nurse testified that she probably held the child in the heater.

A year later, the court had to step in when neighbors informed the Police that the five children were occasionally left to fend for themselves. When they took charge of the children, Yummy was already a boy filled with scars all over his body, and his anger issues were apparent. There were cigarette burns all over his body; he had welts on his legs which looked scared from being beaten with a belt or electrical cord. However, Lorina denied ever beating her children and claimed the scars were from chickenpox and not cigarette burns. She insisted that she gave Yummy and the other children all the attention required except for some occasional distractions. At age 29, Lorina had been arrested more than 41 times, primarily for prostitution.

While mourning her child, she talked about how Yummy liked fishing and pointed to a bucket in the room that still had a frog he caught in it. She talked about how the boy liked fishing and insisted he was a lovely boy, not the monster people painted him. She claimed he was nice to her and called her "Reen" instead of "Mama" like other kids. She admitted he always blamed her for all his woes. She wondered why the system did not save him by rehabilitating him during one of his numerous arrests, like when he started stealing cars. She wondered why he was not put away and put through therapy.

Yummy's Grandma

From the assessment of the child welfare workers, there were no indications that Lorina could be a parent. In his report to the juvenile court, the psychiatrist who examined Robert Sandifer concluded that *"There is no reason to believe that Lorina Sandifer will ever be able to adequately meet her own needs, let alone to meet the needs of her growing family."* So, in 1986, Yummy and his siblings were placed in the custody of his grandmother, Janie Fields, whom he called "Mama." There was not much difference between Janie Fields and Lorina. The psychiatrist, in his testimony, described Yummy's grandmother as *"a very controlling, domineering, castrating woman with a rather severe borderline personality disorder."*

Neighbors recalled the day Janie Fields moved into the Roseland neighborhood; her apartment was three bedrooms in the two-story building. She moved in with her ten children and about 30 grandchildren, who all lived with her one time or another. They lamented about how dirty and noisy the kids were. Some neighbors at some point launched an unsuccessful campaign to have Janie and her brood removed from the apartments, but it failed. Here's how one neighbor described Yummy and his grandmother, "All those kids are little troublemakers." and "This is the kind of neighborhood where we all look after each other's kids, but they are a rougher breed."

Another neighbor describes Yummy as having multiple personalities. She called him a bully, extortionist, a fierce fighter who took on the bigger kids, notwithstanding their size. He would ask for money, and when he noticed you were scared of him, he would ask you for more. He cursed consistently, burnt cars, stole money, and broke into schools and houses. He was always in trouble with law enforcement, but they could do nothing about him. He just went in and came out as a familiar face. He knew he could not be thrown into jail and took advantage of that knowledge to wreak havoc.

Another neighbor described a different Yummy who just wanted to be loved. He could be really kind if he wanted to. He would use words like, "pardon me," "excuse me," and "thank you." His love for animals and basketball was obvious. He also had a way with bicycles- people talked about how he once merged two bicycles to form one. When he was alone, he was a different person; a normal, friendly kid, but all that went out the window when he was in a group.

Yummy was a small kid who had eyes for big cars like Cadillacs and Lincolns. He knew how to drive very well, which explains why he stole many cars at his age and burnt even more. Occasionally, he would hang out at the local garage learning about cars and how to repair them. At some point, when he was reported to his grandmother for throwing things at cars, all she did was yell at him in the presence of everybody, and by the next day, he was back at it.

Yummy's chances of living beyond the age of 12 dropped drastically when he joined the Black Disciples. The BDs with membership numbering around 30 to 40 people per dynasty are constantly recruiting underage boys like Yummy. There's always something to do for the gang. It ranges from drug running to car theft, burglary, extortion, prostitution, gambling, and card fraud in the gang. According to the police, the gangs use these underaged kids and teenagers as drug runners because they know they cannot be prosecuted when they are arrested.

While carrying out all these criminal responsibilities for the gang, it is clear that these young people will not live long before they are gunned down by either their fellow gang members or another rival gang. According to one teenage Black Disciples gang member, you are regarded as a senior citizen if you get to 19. If you make it past that alive and out of jail, you have indeed lived a good life. The gang member further described how these little ones are always willing to make a name for themselves and enjoy favors from the seniors who make them do their dirty work.

Relationship With the Law

In the last year and a half to his death, Yummy averaged one felony per month. Throughout his brief lifetime, he committed 23 felonies and five misdemeanors. Despite his frail and tiny size, he was never intimidated by lawyers, nor did he fear the courtrooms. He was already familiar with all the processes and procedures. In most instances, he knew how the whole drama would end. One former public defender who represented him described his demeanor as unintimidated and relaxed. *"It was like he was just sitting there waiting for a bus,"* she said.

In the fall of 1993, Yummy was checked into the Lawrence Hall Youth services that run homes for troubled teenagers. By February, he had escaped back to his grandmother's house, and by June, he was detained for two weeks in a separate facility. In July, he and his cousin traveled for a church event to Six Flags Great America, an hour north of the city. His cousin explained how Yummy could not get on most rides because of his size and age. On another occasion, one neighbor took Yummy and twelve other kids to see a crime movie. After the movie, one cop asked Yummy not to return with the other kids in the future because he was fighting with other kids and making trouble throughout the movie. In August, he was charged with burglary in a different case. By August 28, he fired the fatal bullet that hit and killed Shavon Dean.

The Shooting of Shavon Dean

On that Sunday evening, Yummy and some gang members were out on a revenge mission to shoot some Gangster Disciples. They came across these boys in a public place, and they had no option other than to shoot at them. Yummy opened fire with a 9-millimeter semiautomatic pistol. He shot at several boys, including his targets, but no one died. They all ran for their lives. However, a stray bullet from Yummy's gun hit a young girl, Shavon Dean, who died on the spot. Yummy and his buddy fled the spot instantly. Shavon, who had been with her parents all day, only stepped out to walk her friend home, but she never made it back.

Gangs shooting each other was common in the neighborhood, but this was too much for the community to bear, mainly because the young lady never belonged to any gang. How the shooting was carried out suggests that Yummy was acting under instruction and trying to score some points or doing it for some cash bonus. One victim of the shooting, Sammy Seay, who was struck in the hand, had this to say, *"I hit the ground. It was the second or third shot before I knew I had been shot. So I got up, and I just ran, trying to save my life.``* He was lucky. Shavon never got the chance.

Hunting Yummy

The police swooped into the community to fish out the killer. Meanwhile, gang members helped Yummy hide in safe houses and abandoned structures for three days while the authorities intensified the pressure to fish out the killer. The Black Disciple leadership felt the heat; they did not want the shooting tied to them. Reporters traveled from all over the country to cover Shavon's death and, in the process, narrowed their focus on gang activities and the Black Disciples. George Knox, a gang researcher at Chicago State University, had this to say about Yummy on the run, *"He was like a trapped animal with everyone after him. He was the hunter, and then he was the prey."*

After three days of being on the run, Yummy called his grandmother and told her he was coming to turn himself in. Maybe at that point, he no longer felt the gang's protection was sufficient to keep him safe. He told his grandmother he would be at 95th Street, but he was no longer there when she got there.

Another account recalled that he showed up on a neighbor's porch, shaken and pleading with them to help him call his grandmother to turn himself in; he even asked if they could pray together. Before the neighbor who went to make the call came back, Yummy was gone. It seems the gang got to him before anyone else. Derrick Hardaway, 14, and his brother Cragg, 16, both honor students and members of the Black Disciples, had been ordered to "take care" of the problem Yummy created for the gang. The gang leaders feared Yummy's arrest would expose their drug activities to the authorities. Hence, they sent the two brothers to fix the problem. They caught up with Yummy and promised to help him escape out of town. He followed them as they drove him to a railroad underpass, a dark tunnel marbled with gang graffiti where they shot him from behind. Again, like Shavon, he did not have the chance to fight for his life.

Yummy and Shavon Were Both Victims

The deaths of Shavon and Yummy happened 14 days apart, and it beamed the light on gang activities in "Chicagoland" at the time, but how long will this continue? I guess only time will tell because the gangs are still there. They are still using underage kids for their dirty work. The Hardaway brothers were later convicted for the murder of Yummy.

During an interview, the Hardaway brothers were asked why they never gave away the name of the Black Disciple leader who ordered the hit on Yummy. One brother responded to the question about how they were made promises in exchange for their silence. They were promised lawyers, money, and support, but they got nothing. They did not even get letters. They talked about how they had no option but to carry out the gang's order, or they would be next to die. For them, it was about loyalty and a sense of belonging. Cragg Hardaway was sentenced to 60 years for murder and eligible for release in 2024, while Derick, who was sentenced to 45 years, was released in 2016 and currently lives a quiet life with his sister in the same neighborhood.

Chapter Six

Chicago: The Headquarters of Drill Music or Violence?

Over the years, as the violence in Chicago has gone unabated, there seem to have been more questions than answers. Gangster icons like Larry Hoover have been behind bars for decades with no hope of coming out any time soon, especially after Kanye West's move to get him freed failed and President Trump lost his reelection to remain in the White House. David Barksdale is also long dead and gone. There are many gang members wasting away in various facilities across the country due to lengthy prison sentences.

Authorities like the Police, FBI, CIA, and politicians have carried out several sting operations and tried several strategies over the decade to curb the menace of gang activities in Chicago. Still, nothing seems to be having the expected lasting effect. The question is, what is at the root of these outbreaks of violence, and what is fueling it?

According to an illustration by Ma'ayan Rosenzweig, which was obtained from the ABC News website, titled *"Hidden America: Don't Shoot I Want to Grow Up"* here are some 2012 Statistics surrounding gang violence in Chicago.

- By October of 2012, the murders in Chicago were 419. The murder rate that year was almost 4 times higher than New York City and more than 2.5 times higher than Los Angeles. However, Chicago is 3 times smaller in population size than New York City and twice as small as Chicago's population.
- In Chicago, in 2012, there was a 24.7% increase in homicide deaths from shootings since the previous year.

- Chicago had the highest number of homicides among cities with populations of 1 million.
- There are 100,000 gang members vs. 12,000 cops in Chicago.
- More than 40% of all homicides in major cities from 2009 to 2011 were gang-related.
- Gang members were responsible for 61% of all homicides in 2011, up from 58.1% in 2010.
- Chicago's official gang count was 59.
- Chicago had a 25% increase in gang activities from 2009 to 2012.
- There was a 40% increase nationally in gang activities from 2009 to 2011
- Average for gang factions: High school age - around 16 to 19. However, there are cases of underage kids between 11 to 14.
- In Chicago, Black males between the ages of 17 and 25 with prior arrest history are most likely to murder victims or be accused of murder.
- 419 people were killed in Chicago; more than the 259 U.S. soldiers killed in Afghanistan.

When the comparison between war-torn Iraq and the City of Chicago started, many thought it was an extreme comparison and possibly overstretching the situation in Chicago, but the numbers don't lie. Over the weekend, July 4, 2014, 84 people were victims of shootings in Chicago; 14 of those victims died from their wounds. That was not the first time that year in the same city.

Over the Easter holiday of the same year, 45 people were shot, and it went on like that, unending. 6 out of those 45 victims were just kids under the age of 15. They were all in a playground where they had gone to attend an Easter service. According to eyewitnesses, a car full of young men carrying semi-automatic guns pulled up and asked one of the boys if he was a member of a particular gang. Still, before he could have the chance to say anything, they started shooting and drove off, leaving chaos, injuries, and death behind.

Apparently, that weekend, a virtual fight started on Facebook, leading to a completely unrelated shooting. Two friends, Jordan Means and Anthony Bankhead, ages 16 and 18, respectively, were involved in a social media fight with a 30-year-old man. In keeping up with his online threat, the man allegedly traced them to their location and killed them.

In a separate incident on the same weekend, two other men were shot and killed in their car with kids between 3 and 7. Although the kids had no physical injuries, they will join the number of mentally scarred soldiers who returned from war and are struggling with Post Traumatic Stress Disorder (PTSD). The incidents on this weekend were followed by another where 37 people were shot with four brutally injured.

James Comey, who was FBI Director at the time, believed that what was happening in Chicago resulted from the gang culture deeply rooted in the city. Still, Chicago Police Superintendent Garry McCarthy believed it was more about gun control than gang culture. The police boss believed that changes could not be expected until something was done about the guns. He explained further how his department had seized more than 1,500 illegal firearms that year, but all the people arrested with these guns were back in the streets in no time, not learning anything about how dangerous carrying a gun can be to them.

In bolstering his point, McCarthy reminded everyone about Hadiya Pendleton, the 15-year-old girl who performed at President Obama's second inauguration but was killed by a stray bullet in 2013, barely a few days after her performance. He lamented that her killers were free to roam the streets even though they were convicted of being in possession of illegal firearms two months prior. He believed that if they had been put into jail, the young lady might still be alive today. Others argue that if the young men were not gang members in the first place, they would not have needed to carry guns. McCarthy concluded by discussing how the Chicago Police Department adopted a wide range of strategies to control gang-related violence.

Ronald Hayes, a 17-year-old teenager who should have been graduating high school as the first in his family, was one of the many victims shot dead in 2014. Ronald had promised to take his mother to prom because she never had the opportunity to attend one. That mother is only left with a painful memory because her son was gunned down while shoveling snow in front of a neighbor's house.

In recent years, another victim of gun and gang violence was Gakirah Barnes, who was killed in revenge for the killing of Odee Perry. On that list, we have Lil Jay and Lil JoJo, who were killed by a stray bullet the day after dissing Chief Keef in his music video. Keef's cousin Mario BigGlo, too, was killed that year. The list goes on.

The shootings and killings happening in Chicago have since gone beyond gang rivalry. Rap has been added to the equation. There is an increase in the number of young men going into Drill rap, mostly because they want to outperform the other group or diss them. It is not just music; it is more of music imitating the lifestyle of these young people. The street had always been divided between the Black Disciples and the Gangster Disciples, but now we have a further divide between OTF, 300, GBE, and Tookaville.

Since Chief Keef rose to prominence with his Drill music from his grandmother's basement, every rival Drill rapper has been trying to "out-rap" him and his group, and this has led to more shootings and killings. We are going to be looking at these rivalries and the death of some of the individuals in these groups.

OTF, 300, and GBE Music Labels and Crews

Only the Family (OTF) is believed to be the brainchild of Lil Durk, who is also a member of the street gang the Black Disciples. However, in an interview with Music Choice, the rapper explained how it all started. *"OTF is 'Only The Family.' It was just a lot of us that hang out for real. The rapping came along, we was like 'We need to make up a rap group.' That's when they made their GBE... and 300 was just everybody."* Durk told Karen Civil of Music Choice.

He explained how the group was just a collection of fellow gang members who enjoyed the company of one another and hung out a lot together. According to him, they were not all rappers, but they did everything together. Several members of the OTF are also from the same notorious Chicago street gang, the Black Disciples. King Von was also a member of the OTF.

In a Facebook post that went viral in 2013, Lil Durk sent a message to his fans from a page with the name "Gbe Lil Durk," saying, *"To all my Fans im not with Gbe No More i cant change my name once I made my page.. #OTF."* We can only conclude that he was previously with the Glory Boyz Entertainment (GBE) crew.

Below are some of the artists, current and deceased, who identify with the OTF music label.

Current Rappers

- Lil Durk
- Memo600
- Doodie Lo
- JusBlow600
- Slimelife Shawty
- Lil Mexico
- Mo Boona
- Chief Wuk
- MJ0.6
- THF Zoo

- Booka600
- OTF OnGod
- OTF Dre2x
- Rondonumbanine
- Lil Varney
- Tortur3 T
- OTF Perris
- OTF Black
- Hypno Carlito
- OTF Jetski
- C3
- Diego

Deceased Artists
- King Von (deceased)
- OTF NuNu (deceased)
- OTF Dthang (deceased)
- Yung Tory
- LA Capone (deceased)

On the other hand, Glory Boyz Entertainment (GBE) was started by Chief Keef as part of his signing with Interscope Records. Keef owned 40%, while his manager Rovan Manuel owned another 40%. The remaining 20% was shared between Fredo Santana, Keef's cousin, Alonzo Carter, an uncle of Keef's, and Anthony H. Dade. The music label which has been active since 2011 would later sign more of Keef's relations and associates like Lil Reese, Fredo Santana, and Producer Young Chop.

The label released Keef's, *"Finally Rich"* around Christmas in 2012 and was preparing to release an album and mixtapes by Lil Reese in 2013, but in a New Year 2014 announcement, Keef said that Glory Boyz Entertainment had ceased to exist and that he was starting a new one called Glo Gang. However, it would turn out to be only a name change.

Below are some of the artists under GBE dead and alive;

Current Artists

- Chief Keef
- Tadoe
- Ballout
- Lil Flash
- Terintino
- Mane Mane
- SmokeCamp Chino
- Jusglo

Former Artists (Dead and Alive)

- Fredo Santana, died in 2018
- Blood Money, Killed in 2014
- Lil Reese
- Capo, Killed in 2015
- Tray Savage, Killed in 2020
- Snap Dogg
- SD
- Rocaine
- Gino Marley
- Stunthard Buda

The rivalry between 300 and Tookaville has left many dead in its wake and others wasting away in prisons, but what hurts more is the families left behind to bear the pain. There's no end to the losses of these families who have lost kids and adults to these fights.

It's sad to know that these rival groups were previously buddies and all grew up together. For example, Lil Durk, along with other drill rappers, was featured in the amateur music video that brought Chief

Keef to prominence. They were all kids jumping back and forth in the video, smoking weed, and wielding guns. Unfortunately, there was tension between Lil Durk and Chief Keef that slip Glo Gang from OTF.

Many have also blamed social media for fueling the tension and bloody rivalry between these groups. It's commonplace to find hashtags like #GDK which means Gangster Disciple Killer, and #BDK, Black Disciple Killer, on social media. These kids start a fight online and follow it up by tracking down their rivals to where they hang in real life and shoot them down.

Joseph Coleman, Aka Lil JoJo - A Talent Lost to a Reprisal Attack

Joseph Coleman, aka Lil JoJo, grew up in the Chicago projects where he joined the Gangster Disciples. He was a committed member of the gang and a true believer in the leadership of Larry Hoover. JoJo belonged to the 068 Brick-squared set of GD. He made several rap songs dissing Chief Keef and the 300 set of the Black Disciples. His songs include Put in Work, Tied Up, Shit is Real, Real Dope, BDK, and A Got Dat Sack.

The shooting and killing of Lil JoJo sparked further debate about the role of gangs, guns, social media, and Drill music in Chicago. A bitter rivalry between Chief Keef and Lil Durk and their followers reached a new height with the release of a remix that dissed and warned of deadly revenge for the murder of Lil JoJo. This song further heightened the tense atmosphere. It threatened more bloodshed in the streets as rival rap groups attacked each other on social media.

Lil JoJo's murder has opened up the debate over Chicago Drill music and there were calls for censorship by the record label signing and distributing this content to curb this violence. According to the Chicago Police Department, there was a 38% increase in homicide cases in the South Side when Lil JoJo was killed.

Lil JoJo's end started like typical beef. Someone had posted a short video of how a kid was rejoicing as he watched Chief Keef being released from prison. The boy rapped Keef's song along as he exclaimed and rejoiced over the release of Keef. That video went viral in a short time, and people who did not know Keef and Drill music started to ask about him. At the time, Chief Keef had only a few videos under his name. They included "3Hunna," which was a reference to his gang, the Black Disciples.

Keef's video later went viral and created a lot of buzz on social media about this new entrant into the rap world. His screen presence, charisma, and a touch of danger endeared many people to him as they watched his video. Little did many know that it was a one-take video from his grandmother's room. The " I Don't Like" video quickly gathered more than 16 million YouTube views at the time.

In no time, celebrity rapper Kanye West did a remix of "I Don't Like." that further pushed Keef's popularity to new heights, such that several recording companies wanted to sign him up. It is important to note that all these companies were not bothered about the rising star's gang affiliations even as Chicago gained national and international attention for the rise in murders. Eventually, Keef settled for Interscope music and signed his first for $3 million. According to Keef, he chose Interscope because they were speaking his language. What that means is left for everyone to guess.

Only a few blocks away, Lil JoJo was working hard to deflate Chief Keef's growing popularity on new turf by starting a rap fight like what we had with Biggie Smalls and Tupac Shakur, in the East Coast versus West Coast style. JoJo posted several videos mocking Keef and the Black Disciple gang. Some of his posts included, "3HunnaK, meaning "3Hunna Killer." Lil JoJo belonged to the Gangster Disciple, who labeled themselves as BDK (Black Disciple Killers). Lil JoJo and his friends posted videos of themselves waving AK47s and Tech 9s in tandem with the rhythm of the beat while dissing Keef. Additionally, one of the posts reads, "*These n---as 300, bet we BDK.*"

The full interpretation of that is, *"these niggas claim to be Black Disciples, but we are Black Disciple Killers."*

Lil JoJo's brother, Cashout, joined in the virtual fight by posting a video of himself and friends imitating them calling Keef's mother and how her old voice cracked over the phone. Later that day, September 4th, JoJo posted a video showing himself and his friend entering Chief Keef's turf as they harassed Keef's buddy Lil Reese. In the video, which was previously available to the public, someone was screaming, saying, "I'm a kill you!"

JoJo would later announce his location in a Twitter post where he mentioned that he would be on 69th Street hanging out with his buddies. At about 7:30 P.M. a car pulled up behind him while he was riding a bike and started shooting at him. Lil JoJo died from injuries sustained from the shooting.

After the murder of Lil JoJo, Chief Keef tweeted, *"Its Sad Cuz Dat Nigg-a JoJo Wanted to be Jus Like Us #LMAO."* There was a public outcry and backlash following the post from Keef. Even his fans attacked him for lack of empathy over the death of a teenager. It was as if all rivalry was set aside to express support for and mourn Lil JoJo. Keef felt the heat from public criticism and later posted another tweet claiming the original post was not from him because his Twitter account was hacked. He further sympathized with and explained that he did not know Lil JoJo but that he was a young guy like him and he had nothing to do with the killing of JoJo.

On the street, JoJo was described as one of the GOAT (Greatest of All Time) of Gangster Disciples due to his commitment and eventual death fighting the course of the gang. He was quite loved by young people his age and fellow gang members.

During his wake, his fans poured in from different parts of the city and beyond for a final glance at JoJo as he was laid to rest. JoJo might have been killed for dissing Chief Keef and the Black Disciples, but that did not stop his fans. One fan blasted JoJo's "3HunnaK" in the funeral home's parking lot while others rapped along in unison. They chanted "BDK....BDK" as loud as they could.

Ahbri Sadin, popularly known on the street as D. Rose, was one of the people Lil Jojo had a virtual fight with before his death. He was arrested and later released for lack of evidence. Ultimately, the killers of Lil JoJo were never apprehended.

Chapter Seven

Ahbir Sadin, D. Rose - Guilty or Not Guilty

Ahbir Sadin, aka D Rose, who got his street name from former basketball star Derrick Rose, was born on June 10, 1996. He is a loyal member of the Black Disciples, a close buddy of Chief Keef, Lil Durk, Fredo Santana, and some key rappers of his time. He is of the 600 set of the BD with a base in the South Side of Chicago. The similarity of his name to the Chicago point guard NBA player implies he's a "shooter" or "Hitta" in street language.

Chief Keef was one of the first and most famous drill rappers to mention D. Rose in his music, saying, "John Madden" said, "600 boy, I ride with those boys - D.Rose boy - My lil bro boy - We gon' blow boy." Chief Keef is a fellow Black Disciple of the 300 Set, also known as the "O' Block."

D. Rose, whose name has featured in several rap lines of Chicago Drill artists, was a rapper himself before he was sentenced to spend 40 years in prison for shooting 14-year-old Venzel Richardson. Ahbir Sadin, along with Lil Reese, Lil Durk, and Chief Keef, was one of the lads who engaged in the virtual fight against Lil JoJo before the latter was later murdered in a drive-by shooting.

According to the Cook County State Attorney's Office, on September 15, 2016, a Cook County Jury convicted Ahbir Sadin, who was 20 years old at the time, for first-degree murder for shooting and killing Venzel Richardson. Court records revealed that the BD loyalist was sentenced to 40 years behind bars. D. Rose, 17 years old when he committed the crime, was featured by name by his compatriots Chief Keef, C-Dai, and RondoNumbaNine at the time of his arrest.

In what looked similar to the JoJo shooting in the description, the prosecution described how Richardson and his friends had just concluded shopping in a nearby convenience store and were headed home two days prior to Valentine's Day, 2014. The friends were walking home South in the 6100 Block of South Vernum when a white minivan pulled up beside them, and the occupant of the front passenger side started shooting.

D. Rose, who was on the run for several weeks before his eventual arrest, was identified by multiple eyewitnesses as the shooter from the minivan. A couple of people described how D. Rose kicked open the side door and fired his handgun at the boys multiple times. According to medical examiners, Richardson suffered four gunshot wounds, including one to the back of his head. Although he managed to escape the shooting scene, he eventually collapsed while fleeing and was pronounced dead when he was found at about 8:25 P.M. He lived at 6400 Block of South St. Lawrence, not far from the shooting scene.

It is unclear what Venzel Richardson and his friend have in common with D. Rose and his fellow gang members. While D. Rose is a loyal Black Disciple and a drill artist, Richardson, was a participant in the Milkwa Challenge. This non-profit program encourages high school students to participate in the political process through elections, solve problems in their communities, and get involved in policy-making programs. In an interview with Homicide Watch Chicago, Jelani McEwen-Torrence, who was Richardson's mentor before he was murdered, talked about how young Richardson would walk his nephew home daily before coming back to be part of the program.

Many people today still believe D. Rose was wrongfully put away for the shooting of Richardson. Since his conviction, there have been several campaigns to plead his case and re-try the case. Two years ago, one Ronnie Boyd started an online petition on www.change.org

petitioning the States Attorney Cook County Chicago Illinois Foxx, and it reads as follows;

"Ahbir Sardin is currently serving a 40-year sentence for a crime he did not commit. People who support and people who don't support him (The rivals to the gang he was allegedly in). All agree on one thing, Sardin did not commit the offense he is being charged with. This petition is a effort to get the case looked at a 2nd time and possibly get justice served for a young man who was giving 40 years at the age of 17 for a crime he did not commit."

Despite the clear grammatical errors, this petition has been signed by almost 12,000 people at the time of writing this part of his story. Fellow gang members and some analysts still argue that D. Rose could not have been responsible for shooting 14-year-old Richardson, but instead, he was being punished for his affiliation with the Black Disciple and his street reputation.

D. Rose was known on the street as a henchman for the Black Disciple who was arrested multiple times for different offenses but managed to escape the long arm of the law. He was once arrested for burglary but never charged in court. After he was released for the murder of Lil Jojo, many felt he got away with murder. Though he was not charged for the shooting of Lil Jojo, he had a target on his back from that time, especially after a post surfaced online claiming he had a hand in the shooting.

Sometime in 2012, after Lil Jojo's murder, another gang member who was a Black Disciple and a member of GBE posted a tweet saying, *"tay jojo thought da same thing into he saw D.rose and Fredo & keke pull up on him boom boom."* Based on Tadoe's affiliation, many took him seriously and concluded that, though he was dissing the Gangster Disciples, he was also letting out insider information. His tweet suggested that Lil Jojo, who died from the shooting, and his injured friends were attacked by D. Rose and Fredo Santana. However, Tadoe later claimed his Twitter account was hacked, and the post did not come from him. It's the same claim Chief Keef made when he had to take down his post. Fredo Santana had made it clear that he had nothing to do with Lil Jojo's shooting.

Several rappers have been campaigning for the release of D. Rose. One of his fellow compatriots, 600Breezy, expressed his unhappiness with D. Rose's verdict. He wrote on his Instagram page, *"He really didn't even do this s**t. He wasn't even there. I hate the system free my brothers this s**t foul. He a innocent man. they doing this because of his street name. S**t ain't right."*

It is essential to point out that many of the Black Disciple rappers who sing "Free D. Rose" as part of their song had the wrong impression that he was convicted of a Triple Homicide. This rumor was started by online commentators and has since gained some prominence. However, it is just a rumor. Ahbir Sardin is in jail for his role in the shooting and murder of Venzel Richardson.

Denied Appeal

In 2019, D. Rose appealed his conviction for the drive-by shooting that led to the death of Venzel Richardson. His defense claimed the trial court was wrong to have overruled his defense's objections to the State's introduction of the names of two other rappers. The rappers in question are D. Rose's Black Disciple buddies, Clint Massey, who goes by the street name RondoNumbaNine, and Courtney Ealy, also known as D-Dai.

In 2016 before D. Rose's trial, both rappers who were also buddies of Chief Keef were arrested, charged, and found guilty of first-degree murder for killing a 29-year-old cab driver, Javan Boyd. Mr. Boyd was killed by the two men in a case of mistaken identity. He was mistaken for a rival gang member the lads fought earlier that night. They were sentenced to almost 40 years each.

The trial judge put an end to D. Rose's appeal because the Jury had heard the testimony about RondoNumbaNine and C-Dai. In his final opinion, Judge Thomas V. Gainer wrote, *"The two rappers were relevant to the course of the police investigation of this offense because, the day before, they and the defendant were stopped by the police in a van that witnesses identified as the same type of vehicle used in this drive-by shooting."*

The defense argued that the testimony relating to D. Rose's affiliation with the Drill rappers was unfair and prejudicial, mainly due to their unrelated murder convictions.

The Judge disagreed with the defense and concluded that *"The connection could only have been possibly prejudicial if a juror had both heard of, and recalled the convictions from six months earlier. Even if we accepted defendant's contention that there were articles and publicity, we could not find the type of saturation that would preclude a fair trial, in the absence of evidence of juror knowledge,"*

D. Rose continues to serve his sentencing while still trying for appeal. His buddies, too, are still out there asking for him to be released. With the whole campaign going on for the freedom of D. Rose, one could wonder if he is the real victim.

Rose Converts to Islam

While serving his time, D. Rose embraced and converted to Islam. Below is an excerpt of his exclusive interview with the Black Dawah Network where Hakeem Muhammad, JD, spoke to D-Rose/Ahbir Sardin.

Hakeem Muhammad: As-Salaam Alaikum Brother Ahbir. I hope you got that copy of The Autobiography of Malcolm X we sent you.

D-Rose/Ahbir: Walikum saalam wa rahmatullahi wa barakatuh. Yeah, I have read Malcolm X's Autobiography. InshAllah, I will give it to someone else who I think will benefit.

Hakeem Muhammad: Malcolm X talks about some real stuff in that book, especially when he says, "In the ghettos, the white man has built for us he has forced us not to aspire to greater things but to look to everyday living here for survival." But, his life was transformed by the message of Islam, and I know you have also come to Islam, Alhamdulillah. What would you say Islam has done for you?

D-Rose/Ahbir Sardin: Islam has made my relationship with Allah, subhana wata ala more strong. It made me aware of my morals and why I felt the way I did in the past, and Islam urges me to be kind and show love and compassion. Even now, fasting humbles me and gives me the perspective that I need. Islam has helped me a lot. Islam is the guidance of righteousness and livelihood. Islam assures me that I'm not supposed to be heartless.

Hakeem Muhammad: We know the prison system is white supremacy's tool to re-enslave Black people. What are you doing to stay strong behind enemy lines?

D Rose/Ahbir Sardin: Reading the Qu'ran and going to Jummah every time. It strengthens my faith and doing tasbih. I like to hear talks about Allah, s.w.a, and the Prophet Muhammad. Peace be upon him. Being among the Muslims, it strengthens me.

Hakeem Muhammad: I know you were deeply involved in Chicago's Drill rap scene. In a lot of those songs, we see Black brothers threatening their "ops." Given the history of how Black communities in Chicago were systematically oppressed and marginalized, what would you say to the proposition that white supremacy is our greatest "op"?

D Rose/Ahbir Sardin: I'm aware of the injustices and the fact that the Constitution was made when we were slaves, and the history of Jim Crow. I'm aware of the Willie Lynch syndrome. My consciousness is there.

Hakeem Muhammad: Definitely, I think it is through Islam that we are gonna get rid of the Willie Lynch mentality. We need to bring a Mosque to your hood in O-block where our brothers in the streets can learn about Islam.

D Rose/Ahbir Sardin: Opening a Mosque near that hood is great, and I would love it, like I would be so thankful, brother.

The Real Victims

Laveta Richardson, the mother of Venzel Richachson, found out about her son's death how no mother should ever hear about the death of their child.

She was in her home at about 10 P.M that night when she heard a knock on her front door. It was her niece who had seen "RIP Venzel" scrolling on TV under the main news. She came to check on Laveta to find out what was happening. Laveta did not know that her 14-year-old boy had been shot dead just a few blocks away from their Woodlawn home on his way home, along with his friend, who also suffered gunshot wounds. She dashed to 6100 block of South Vernon Avenue, the shooting scene, but on arrival, the boy's body had already been moved, and the police asked her to wait in a car as she continued to ask questions of anyone who cared to listen.

In her own words, *"I never wanted to be like the mothers on TV that are crying because their babies got shot,"* Richardson said Thursday as she began to break down and sob. *"And now I'm a victim. They shot my baby in the head."*

By the next day, friends and family gathered in her 6,400 blocks of South St. Lawrence Avenue to mourn with Laveta. You could feel her pain as she struggled to speak in between tears while her sister supported her. *"I wanted to keep my baby home, but you can't keep your baby in the house all the time,"* she said. *"They go outside. You can't keep them in forever."*

According to Police, Venzel was the main target of the shooting because he had gang affiliation with one of the two main gangs in Chicago. They believed his shooting was a result of a social media feud or a reprisal attack. However, Venzel's family denied the teenager was a member of any gang. They believed he was a victim of a bad neighborhood that kept deteriorating daily.

Denise Richardson, Laveta's sister, expressed concern about how the police and the media were trying to write off her nephew's murder as just another gang-related shooting. *"It's probably going to get, like, 20 minutes of attention. Then they'll forget about it and move on to the next case,"* she said.

"We don't want Venzel to be known how the police are portraying him — as a gangbanger," said his aunt, Denise Richardson. *"We don't want him to be another statistic, just lying out there in the snow. Dead. Just another black kid. 'Oh, he's in a gang.'"*

Venzel was a freshman at Dunbar Vocational Career Academy, 3000 S. King Drive. He had a great interest in politics and English; like his friends, he liked football, playing video games, and making amateur videos with his friends. He had dreams of attending a school in Chicago so that he could stay close to his mother.

The mother of three expressed her concerns about the funeral cost for her son because she had lost her job the previous year. *"I used to sit my son in front of the television and say, 'Look Venzel, look at what this mom is going through. ... I want you to be careful out there. Don't go down certain streets.'... Now my baby is gone."*

Chapter Eight

RondoNumbaNine & C-Dai – A Criminal Collaboration

Who is RondoNumbaNine?

RondoNumbaNine was born in 1996 as Clint Massey from the South Side of Chicago, Illinois. Like many young men born in the Chicago projects in his time, Rondo was part of the Drill movement. He is pretty famous on the streets and well known in the Black Disciples, where he was a member, and to their rival the Gangster Disciples. As a loyal member of the 600 set of Black Disciples, he has strong ties with famous drill artists like Chief Keef, Lil Reese, Lil Durk, Fredo Santana, Tay 600, La Capone, C-Dai, and D. Rose. He has also collaborated with most of them.

Rondo's unique style of music tends to focus more on his daily lifestyle in the projects, the challenges that poverty brings, his struggles with the authorities, the rivalry with opposing gang members, and virtual beef between the various factions on the street. It's a common sight in his music videos to see himself and buddies showing off gang signs and praising the Black Disciples or OTF while dissing their rivals with disdain and unprintable names. Lil Jojo and Fly Boy Gang (FBG) are some instances of rivals that have been attacked in RondoNumbaNine's song, but the Gangster Disciples and the artists from that side of the divide are most often the target of these disrespectful lyrics.

Unfortunately, the beef and dissing that Rondo has been involved in have not all ended on Twitter or other social media platforms. Some have been taken to the streets, where they ended with violent shootings leading to injuries and deaths.

Chicago is a place where dreams of young men and women die due to ongoing murder cases that started from lyrical beefs or social media. Rondo was involved in one of such cases, and he bagged a lengthy prison sentence due to his involvement.

On September 26, 2013, La Capone, Rondo's close buddy, was added to the numerous death by drive-by shootings in Chicago. He was a member of the same 600 set of the Black Disciples who could have been great if only he had lived longer. La Capone was gunned down outside the studio after a recording session, and a few hours after the shooting, he was pronounced dead. Rondo later released a song in honor of Capone titled, "Trap Spot." Other songs released by Rondo include "Shooters," "Play for Keeps," "among several others. There are also mixtapes like "I'm Up Next," released in 2012 with 12 tracks and has enjoyed millions of downloads.

Who is C-Dai?

C-dai was officially named Courtney Ealy but also liked to be called 22Shotz. He was born on October 9, 1994. Not much is known about C-dai and his family other than his brother Edai. He is a member of the 600 Black Disciples and friends with RondonumbaNine, D. Rose, Fredo Santana, Chief Keef, Lil Durk, La Capone, and Tay 600.

C-dai's Career

In December 2013, Fredo Santana mentioned on his Twitter handle that he had signed C-dai to his record label, the Savage Squad Records. Before his arrest and incarceration, the young rapper had released some videos on YouTube, including, "My N*ggaz" and,

"Bail Out," which featured his close ally RondoNumbaNine. He was also featured in RondoNumbaNine's "Go Crazy" and "Get Some Gwuap."

Fellow Black Disciples gang members also like to pay tribute to C-dai and his contribution to the course of the gang in the community. In a song "Play for Keeps," featuring RondoNumbaNine, La Capone said, "Cdai got 22 shots ni*ga - add 8 more, that's a mop ni*ga."

C-dai's other songs include "Sucka," "Glocks N Chops," "Shooters," "Pay for Keeps," "Just to let you know," and "Man Down."

The Boys' Unceremonious TV Debut

In late 2012, the reality TV show, "Tru TV," carried out an experiment in the Englewood area of Chicago. They left a black sedan car unattended, but the police and other crew members were watching in and outside the car from a distance.

Within a few minutes of leaving the car unattended, multiple boys and girls from the neighborhood invaded and started stealing and looting the car. The hidden camera revealed that they were boys from the 300 and 600 crews of the Black Disciples. The looting became uncontrollable within a short time as boys and girls moved in and out of the car, searching and taking things away.

Even the baby carrier at the back seat was not spared as it was quickly removed and taken away. While the crew watched, one guy looked for and found the car keys, while another one drove the car away from the open location where it was parked to a quieter location where they started to vandalize the car. The action happening in and outside the car became too much for the watching crew to handle- they had to intervene to stop the looting immediately.

By the time the TV crew arrived with about five police vehicles escorting them, the boys had already turned out the back seats and had started taking things away. Present at the point of this looting was C-dai, whose name was mentioned by another gang member a couple of times. Other members of the Black Disciples who were involved in the looting and vandalization of the bait car were RondoNumbaNine, D. Rose, La Capone, and Tay600.

The video from that episode of "Bait Car" by "Tru Tv" went viral when it aired, and a lot of the names and faces of the Drill rappers in the video were recognizable. Chief Keef even commented after the episode aired, saying, *"Dey got dem Oblock boyz on here #MyNiggasCantBelieveIt Teen Mob – Bait Car,"* on his Twitter handle.

Rondo's Career

Under normal circumstances, Rondo would have been one of the greatest Drill rappers of all time by now. He had everything working for him, and he was on the path already before his dream was cut short. As of 2012-2014, he was one of the most talked-about Drill rappers out of the Chicago Drill era with songs like, "Hang Wit Me," and "Ride," where he features Lil Durk. Both the one he sang alone and the one featuring Lil Durk have combined YouTube views of more than 30 million. "Play for Keeps" would be Rondo's biggest song so far.

He featured his late friend La Capone in this one, and it currently has more than 49 million views on YouTube. Some have gone ahead to describe it as one of the best songs to come out of the Chicago projects. Also, many believe Rondo's loud and yelling style of rapping might have been imitated by rappers like 6ix9ine. Rondo was designed and made to be up there with the best of them from Chicago, and then all of the rap worlds, but his bad decisions truncated his rise to glory, and no one can say precisely how high he would have risen or if he would ever come close to what he used to be.

Rondo and C-Dai's Rap Sheet

How did Rondo end up with a bleak future? The first time he would appear on the police's radar, he was the subject of an investigation. It started in December 2013, when he appeared on his Instagram showing off a rocket launcher and captioned it, "coolin id with my baby!!" The pictures immediately went viral beyond Chicago and almost nationwide. The Chicago police launched an investigation into his activities alongside other government crime-fighting units at the federal level.

As part of their investigation, the Chicago police took it upon themselves to inform the residents of what was going on. They sent out a letter to the residents and included Rondo's picture holding the rocket launcher. They included his address and full name. Rondo was later pressured to delete the post and claimed he was fooling around and never had a real rocket launcher. Social media fact-checkers later confirmed that the "AT4" the young rapper was showing off had a blue ribbon around it, meaning it was not able to fire a live round; instead, it was either for practice only or props. Rondo was never arrested for this incident, so we can assume he never posed any real threat to anyone with that weapon.

On February 21, 2014, three months after the rocket launcher incident, Rondo's activities were once again in the interest of a police investigation, only this time he was in real trouble. He was 17 years old when he attended a party with a couple of friends at the Wentworth Gardens Housing project in South Side Chicago. Other friends present at the same party were T'Keyah Herbert, Jasmine Brown, Kaprice Johns, Lil Boo, Tay 600, and C-Dai. They had all spent the night partying as they usually would, but it was RondoNumbaNine, C-Dai, and Herbert that left the others behind. It was gathered that after those three left in Herbert's van, Johns got into an argument with Tay600, Lil Boo, Brown, and some ladies over song choices being played at the party.

As the argument continued, a gunshot was fired into the air to calm the situation, but Johns thought the shot was directed at her or her crew. She later departed from the party with Brown, Tay 600, and Lil Boo. On their way back from the party, Tay600 called C-Dai and explained the altercation that happened and how someone shot at them. The two groups then agreed to meet at Wendy's where they picked up a mutual friend and gang member, D. Rose, who had been waiting in a red car. Rondo and C-Dai later joined D. Rose in his car, and they drove back to the venue of the party at Wentworth Gardens. Herbert and another group that had Tay600, Lil Boo, Johns, and Brown followed them closely. They went in search of the person who fired the shot at their crew.

As the convoy drove close to 38th and Princeton, they saw a man sitting alone in his car parked and waiting. All three cars went to make an immediate U-turn, then Rondo and C-Dai exited the red car D. Rose was driving and rushed toward the man through the passenger side of his car while he was still waiting but now wondering who these people were and what they wanted with him. After a brief conversation, seven shots were fired at the man right inside his car. Rondo and C-Dai ran back to their vehicle, and all three cars drove off the scene. The man in the car was Javad Boyd, a cab driver who was there to pick up someone who lived in the Wentworth Gardens project. He did not know anything about the party and certainly had not met the crew before. He was probably at the wrong location at the wrong time.

This could have been another case of an unknown drive-by shooting in the Chicago projects, but it was not to be. Police investigators gradually started piecing together their evidence to unravel the killing of Javad Boyd. The first evidence was at the shooting scene, where they found an iPhone; it looked like it was dropped as the shooter fled the shooting scene. That phone was later discovered to belong to C-Dai. The following evidence was C-Dai's fingerprint, which he left on the passenger side of Boyd's car. The last and most important evidence was that the whole shooting was captured by a nearby surveillance camera, which showed RondoNumbaNine and C-Dai fleeing after killing Boyd.

It did not take long for the Chicago Police Department to pick up Rondo from his Englewood home and charge him for the murder of Javad Boyd and hold him on a $2 million bail. C-Dai, his partner in crime was also arrested a few days later at Chief Keef's Northfield mansion and was charged for the same crime. While awaiting their trial, the two men were held in the County Cook jail for more than two years.

The prosecutor's office felt good about this case because they seemed to have the two men where they wanted them. The evidence was overwhelming, and it was clear the two shooters would be going away for a long time. In addition to the pieces of evidence, which included C-Dai's iPhone, his fingerprint, and the surveillance camera showing the two men running off from the shooting scene, all the ladies who witnessed the incident that night gave the police the same story.

For his part, word on the street is that C-dai had murdered more than three people before he was eventually put away for the shooting of Mr. Boyd. In the song, "Man Down," he talked about a shooting that led to a murder he allegedly committed. His social media handle 22 Shotz is also an indication of some of the shootings he has been involved with, but he was never convicted of any.

In 2012 C-dai was convicted of a felony robbery, and he was sentenced to two years' probation. At the time of his arrest for the shooting of Boyd, he had two violations on the case.

Who Snitched?

There have been talks of snitching on the streets, especially around RondoNumbaNine snitching to the police about what happened that February night. Several people have called out Rondo for snitching to the police and confessing his role in the shooting of Boyd. These allegations make the rounds and grow stronger because many believe Rondo must have sold out his buddy C-dai in his bid for early release.

It is alleged that given the evidence available to the prosecutors, Rondo could not have been an active shooter that night. However, his fingerprint was present at the shooting scene, just as he was also seen in the surveillance video. Furthermore, the real cause of Javad Boyd's death was gunshot wounds, and C-dai was the only active shooter that night. Rondo has been pleading his case for a while now with support from outside the prison walls, and it's looking more likely that he would get out early, but the same cannot be said of C-dai.

Furthermore, there were rumors that Tay600 also snitched on the two friends, and paperwork to back the evidence surfaced on the internet, but it was never confirmed. The same rumor made the rounds again in 2020, and this time it seemed more convincing than years before.

In his defense, Tay600 has continuously denied snitching on any of his friends. He claimed the paperwork making the rounds on the internet was fake and possibly made by a fan. He has asked anyone who has evidence to bring it out for him to see. Tay600 himself was in jail for the better part of the time when he was alleged to have snitched.

C-dai and Breezy saw court papers from Rondo's lawyers that said Tay600 testified that Rondo was the active shooter. Other Drill rappers who called out Tay600 for snitching include Lil Durk, Breezy, and Lil Reese. We don't want to say anyone is a rat without paperwork to prove it. We are just sharing the information without knowing whether it is true or false.

In March 2016, Breezy, a mutual friend to both friends and fellow gang member, wrote about the sentencing of the two young men on his Instagram, *"I don't even know what to say bro… I love y'all for life. Real 600's real n***z for life."* He added further, this time via his

Twitter handle, *"9 couldn't even look me in my face Cdai just dropped his head and walked out I'm sick to my stomach."*

Rondo's Road to Freedom

Rondo was 17 years old when he was sentenced to 39 years in prison for his role on the night Boyd was shot and killed. He is not scheduled to be released until 2056, but he is currently working on his appeal.

Lil Durk has been talking about how he is working on helping Rondo with his appeal and how he intends to set up a future for the fellow OTF and Black Disciple rapper. He talked about how they have been working tirelessly, back and forth with the lawyers, and that it was looking good for Rondo. Lil Durk reiterated his confidence in a series of tweets, saying, *"If I told y'all #9 a be home this year, would you believe me !!"*

The status of the appeal is unclear at the time of writing this story. However, RondoNumbaNine has been tweeting a lot about his incarceration and other issues. Below are some of them.

On June 4, 2018, he sent out this through his **@rondonumbanine** handle, *"Just spent 25 on a lawyer! Add 3 zeros to that, tell Durk he is the realist for that told me this shit deeper than rap..."*

On July 26, 2021, he tweeted, *"Booka pay for rose lawyer gave money to Cdai lawyer pretty sure he do everything for Mac and bite down to plus his family why take risk when he high commodity and he to official?? Stay in yo element brother to gown to real #Facts Mr. Loyal"*

The same day he posted another tweet *"Okay C Murda BG, I'm 24 been jammed 8 years neva sold drugs i'm the real of a chi raq trench baby from the south side Englewood area steve drive to be specific. Yea think about…#RN4L*

Yet another tweet on the same day, *"why my return mean so much? First off cuz I'm really that, and I come back all my brothers that's gone comeback (attached), all them knew Wassup wit me and I know wassup wit them, so I ain't got no choice but to do that LA Vroy Fredo Nsuki Jmoney Pluto Steve YEA."*

On July 29, 2021, he posted, *"I'm tell y'all whats the realest form of loyalty... Honor and real beyond everything value solid foundation and genuine vibes on the daily I can show you how to be a loyal real one."*

On July 31, he tweeted, *"When I got jamed for this case I didn't even think about the charge I thought about leaving my family smirk and my brothers i was in my head laying in my cell I aint wanna talk to nobody I was strong but hurt! I knew I was gone lose a lot of people I was preparing!"*

RondoNumbaNine, like his buddy D. Rose, continues to fight for his freedom from behind bars.

C-Dai's Cry for Help - Another Case of Abandonment

Like the Rondo situation, Cdai, too, has claimed that his 600 crew abandoned him. He claimed he hadn't had any form of support, money, or visitation from his buddies. Instead, it's the fans who have been showing their support and sending him money. C-dai stated in an interview with VLAD TV, *"That's more than n***as that I knew for 20-plus years, you know. So that sh*t crazy, I definitely appreciate the love from my fans."* Cdai further buttresses his loyalty to his crew, stating, *"I can never regret the sh*t I did. You know, I just regret the sh*t I did for all the wrong n***as."*

C-dai was 19 when he was eventually arrested at 1800 Block of Willow Road in Northfield. The court document revealed C-dai's official address as 300 Block of East 60th Street. He was also charged with one count of first-degree murder and was held on a $1 million bond for the murder and probation violation on two unrelated cases like his fellow culprits.

The presiding Judge, Chiampas, further issued a no-contact restriction barring Cdai from interacting with any witnesses or visiting the crime scene and its vicinity. *"You are prohibited from all social media, which means no Facebook, no Instagram, no my-gram, your-gram, I don't care whose it is,"* Chiampas said.

Interestingly, C-dai, who has been a lifelong Chicago resident, lived with his mother, who was a public defender. He was enrolled in GED classes but never saw it through. He was more known on the streets than in educational settings.

C-dai talked extensively about his 600 crew making a lot of money and not sending him any. In that interview, part of the issues he addressed was how RondonumbaNine sat back and watched his lawyer throw him under the bus. in his words, *"Rondo sat next to me in a room full of jurors and [played] innocent while he [threw] me under the bus."*

D. Rose, RondoNumbaNine, and Cdai, who appeared in the "Bait Car" episode, are all cooling off in jail, serving time for different murders. Although they are all fighting their sentencing, no one knows for sure if any of these boys will get out earlier than the time they were given. These men are young Drill rappers languishing in jail for their role in gang activities and street notoriety.

The Victim

With all the ongoing talks about the rapper's release, people seem to be forgetting the real victim, Javad Boyd. Mr. Boyd's life was already one marred by tragedy before he met his unfortunate death at the hands of C-Dai and Rondo.

In June 1994, Javad Boyd was the only survivor of a fire at an apartment building at the former Robert Taylor Homes. His entire family died in the fire except him because he had to be in school as the only child old enough to attend school. His mother's sister managed to escape the fire with her infant and took care of him as hers.

Boyd had only been a livery driver for three weeks driving his unmarked vehicle. Before his untimely death, Boyd was working two jobs to take care of his family.

The lady who was supposed to pay Boyd said she came out and saw all the chaos that had taken place; that was when she screamed and called the police. The spokesperson for Boyd's company says they service the whole of that area, and nothing like that had ever happened to any of their drivers before.

Trina Boyd, who took care of Javad as her own, said all she wanted was justice.

According to family members, Boyd had been in trouble with the law before when he was arrested in 2007 for aggravated vehicular hijacking where he pleaded guilty. However, he remained clean since then. At the time of his shooting, he was working a second job as a food packer in West suburban Woodridge to support his 11-year-old daughter. The clean-cut old-school livery driver enjoyed spending time with his daughter taking her bowling or watching her skate.

Javad Boyd, 28 of the 7400 block of South Chapel Avenue, died less than two hours after arriving at John H. Stroger Hospital of Cook County.

Chapter Nine

TY, Odee, Tooka and KI – 4 Lives Linked by Death

In this chapter, we shall be looking at the lives of 4 young people whose stories are linked together by crime, shootings, and murder. Individually, they are big names on the street and in the Drill world but it is difficult to talk about them separately because of how their stories connect. So, let's get right into it.

Who is Eddrick Walker, aka TY?

Eddrick Tyshawn Walker, also known as 'TY', was born on June 6, 1992, and died on May 21, 2009 when was gunned down by a member of the Gangster Disciples. He lived in 600 block of East Marquette Road. He was the leader of the Black Disciples set, 065 Young Money (064YM), also called, Murder Maryland.

The gang is located on 65th and Maryland on Chicago's Southeast Side. After the death of TY, it was called TYMB (TY You're My Brother), a name adopted by the Young Money gang in honor of Eddrick. The TYMB had issues with the Gangster Disciple sets in the area, mainly the STL/EBT (St Lawrence Boys/Everything But Trap).

A Short Life

The 17-year-old Eddrick Walker was shot in the 6500 block of South Evans Avenue in the West Woodlawn neighborhood. He suffered multiple gunshot wounds in the attack, which happened a little before 10 pm on Tuesday, May 21, 2009. Police think his killing was gang-related and a retaliation by a rival gang over a fight that started online.

On the same day, three other people were killed close to the area Eddrick was murdered. 27-year-old Derrick Armstrong was shot multiple times and taken to Stroger Hospital. He was pronounced dead at 10:19 pm. 19-year-old Bernadette Turner, female, was also shot in the neck. She was taken to Mount. Sinai Hospital where she died on arrival.

Derrick and Bernadette were both sitting in a vehicle when a male figure approached them, opened fire, and fled the scene. The killing happened in the 3000 block of West Van Buren Street in the East Garfield Park neighborhood. That same night, in the 1500 block of North Learnington Avenue in the North Austin neighborhood, 22-year-old Steven Robinson was found dead outside his residence.

Not far from where Eddrick was killed, three men were wounded in a drive-by shooting in 6300 Block of South St Lawrence Avenue. A 28-year-old man was shot in his stomach, and another 22-year-old man was shot in his lower back. They were both taken to Northwestern Hospital, while a 34-year-old man suffered a slight injury to his left arm as a result of the shooting.

Who killed TY?

The grievance between 065YM and STL/EBT started when Eddrick allegedly killed Dalvin, a Blood Street gang (BSG) member, in September 2007. STL/EBT and BSG became allies, and the STL/EBT retaliated. Carl 'C-Ball' Burnette was accused of killing Eddrick. He was a Gangster Disciple member from the STL/EBT.

17-year-old Quinton Glover of 1400 block of West 73rd Street and 22-year-old Centrell Lanier of the 6200 block of South Talmon Avenue were both charged with the murder of Eddrick Walker in

2010. 19-year-old Roderick Brown was also charged with the slaying. Centrell was already serving a 3-year sentence in state prison for unlawful possession of a weapon by a felon. Roderick was on probation in a case involving selling or possessing stolen goods at the time of the shooting.

People suspect that the killing of Shondale Gregory, popularly known as 'Tooka', was related to Eddrick's murder. Through his Facebook handle, 'Fitchmade Ohsixthreesaluteorshoot Fuqboy', Tooka made derogatory comments about Eddrick Walker.

Tooka posts: *Man Muthaf**** need 2 keep our name out dey mouth…muthaf***** shouldnt be lackn…KEEP MA TEAM NAME OUT YALL*

Robin replies: *yhu s.t.l woow, s.t.l k…wat who mad*

Tooka: *ROBIN B***H WATCH UR MOUTH YHU A SKN WHO MAD B***H YHU MAD… S.T.L TILL DHA DEATH OF MEH B**G B***H*

Robin: tooka stop playn with meh you goofey a**, young money till dha world end f***…b***h

Keya: *Tooka Kall Meh Back TookaHunz We Dnt Beat Dha Keyboard Or Symphathizee Fah Silly Kids Kut Dhat Shyt Out*

Tooka: *ROBIN YHU SCARY AS HELL…B***H,S.T.L,E.B.T,A.B.M,JAROCITY IN DHAT ORDER WE GOT SHOOTERS ON DECK ASK T.Y*

These posts were made on Facebook on January 9, 2011, three days before his death. After Tooka's death, the opposing gang members like Chief Keef and King Von made degrading comments about him in their social media posts and rap songs. More about all that in a bit.

Who is Tooka?

Shondale 'Tooka' Gregory was a known affiliate of the Gangster Disciples- one of the many Chicago gang members who was murdered. What makes his case different is how the name 'Tooka' has gone far and wide and is now used as slang and in rap songs. According to Moslidez, Tooka has become one of the most disrespected people in rap history.

Tooka was born and raised in Chicago's most dangerous neighborhood, now known as 'O Block'. Reports say that in O Block, every three hours someone gets shot, and every fourteen hours, someone gets killed.

His father was said to have been killed in 2019, seven years after the young rapper's death. According to The Street Report, *"A 41-year-old man was talking on his cellphone about 5:35 am while walking back to his apartment in the 6500 Block of South Martin Luther King Drive; four people were following him, police said. He made it into his apartment but was shot in the chest and killed. The man was found dead about 5:40 am, according to police. RIP Tooka's daddy".*

Tooka's mother is Dominique Boyd. After Tooka's death, she protested about her son's name being used disrespectfully in different Drill lyrics and spoke about how it upsets her. Tooka also had a brother, Marc 'Lil Marc' Campbell, who was also killed in 2014.

Tooka's Death

On January 12, 2012, young Tooka's life was taken while waiting for a bus. A car pulled up in front of him at the bus stop, a passenger got out, and they began exchanging words. Afterward, the unknown gunman fired multiple shots at Tooka and took off, but the young rapper did not survive the shooting and he was pronounced dead at the scene.

Officially, Tooka's killer was unknown but, on the streets, Odee Perry was believed to be responsible for the shooting, which was revenge for the murder of his gang member. We are only halfway along this circle of killing and revenge that never gets solved by the authorities. It would appear as if the authorities try to wash their hands of these murders once it's clear that they are gang-related. While this may be an assumption at this point, the fact that only a handful of cases have been solved over the years counts for something.

Tooka's Mom Expresses Her Grief

In an interview with Chicago's Dean O Show, Chicago mothers who have lost their children to violence on the streets opened up about how they felt. Tooka's mom begins by explaining her son's death. *"Shondale was 15 years old when he got killed. He was standing on a bus stop coming home from school like a normal child supposed to. On January 12, 2011. I got a call from him at 6:08 telling me he was on his way home, and I got a call from a detective at 6:14 telling me my son was dead".*

When asked about how she feels about her son's reputation and people saying they are smoking on Tooka, she replies, *"He got his nickname from the hospital. They called him attitude, I shortened it up for Tooka… I don't get how they can feel so intimidated by someone who is 15 years old and want to take a person and be making him into a strain of weed. I mean where did that come from? Who smokes on a dead person. It makes me so upset because I mean where do the level of disrespect start. He's already dead. He's not here to do nothing to nobody… I don't get it. People are just so cruel in this world. I don't understand how people could be so cruel."*

She further expresses her pain as it feels like more rappers are disrespecting her son's name.

"My son's been dead 10 years and it's like I still can't get no type of lenient nowhere. You turn around and it feel like [both] the upcoming ones [and]

people that's already in the industry and they don't even know my son. They just went over something somebody else said about my son and it's not fair. It's not fair and that's why I'm here today. I'm gonna give my son a voice. I've been doing it from day one when my son got killed that I didn't want no retaliation, but yet it's ongoing and I want it to stop. I just want it to stop. I just want us to come together as one."

LaSheena Weekly, FBG Durk's mother, also commented on disrespecting the dead in rap songs and uniting mothers of Chicago residents slain by violence. She says, *"What I'm trying to establish now is a round table to bring all the moms together who has lost their children due to the violence due to the stigma that everybody has on Chicago with the smoking the dead people and disrespecting the dead. Hopefully, this movement would stop that and show people's real talent, because if people stop dying, they won't have nothing to rap about. If they're rapping about Drill music so need to show our talents other ways, the talent that we know we have. It shouldn't take nobody to die for you to diss them to\ get leverage or accolades. It never made sense to me."*

Rivalry with The Black Disciples

As part of the rivalry between Chicago gangs, their members sometimes taunt each other via songs and social media, and as the mothers in the previous section stated, it matters little if the rival is dead or alive; the touting never stops. 15-year-old Tooka murdered at a bus stop has now been reduced to weed slang. Drill's founding father, Chief Keef, and Chicago rapper from O Block, King Von, were the pioneers of dissing Tooka in their rap songs.

Chief Keef disrespectfully mentioned Tooka's name in several lines at the start of his career, including the song, '3hunna'. He rapped, *"F**k a Tooka gang b***h I'm 3hunna"*. 3Hunna is a nickname for the Black Disciples gang.

King Von has mentioned the phrase, 'Smoking Tooka' various times in his songs. 'Smoking Tooka' is now synonymous with getting high.

Urban Dictionary defines it as: *"A word used to describe potent marijuana originated after Shondale 'Tooka' Gregory was murdered (smoked) by Chief Keef's crew, Black Disciples. Now 'Smoking Tooka' is used to humiliate Shondale's death."*

King Von rapped in his song, 'All These N****s' released three months before his death,

"Got Tooka in my lungs. I say that every time 'cause he got smoked (He got smoked)". He also released a song called 'How I Rock (Tooka Pack)' where he rapped, "*Drop some, everybody holler, von drop somethin'. But I can't, 'cause all the opps dead, it's hard to drop somethin'. Smokin' on this Tooka pack and it's loud as f**k. Foenem caught Tooka a** getting' off the bus. I know Tooka mad as hell, he probably tired of us. But when I die, find Tooka a** and I'ma beat 'em up."*

Going by how Chief Keef and King Von detested Tooka, people wonder whether Tooka did something to deserve such hate. It's unclear whether they had personal issues with Tooka. On the other hand, the suspicion of Tooka being responsible for the death of one of their own and the fact that Odee Perry was later shot and killed for allegedly shooting Tooka further fueled the bitterness against Tooka and his side of the street gang. Retaliatory shootings and killings are typical on the streets of Chicago and among rival gangs, but none has been as pronounced as the shooting of Tooka. The gangs will not allow Tooka to rest in peace like those who have gone before and after him.

Tooka's name was mentioned so often that other rappers started saying his name. The line, 'Smoking tooka' got so popular that it became a meme. The situation is worsened by the fact that even upcoming rappers within and outside Chicago, who knew very little about young Tooka are dissing his name. For example, Young MA in a show spit bars over a few beats. One line caught the attention of Tooka's close friends. She rapped, *"I smoke hookah like its Tooka blowing jet clouds. And I only get high to bring stress down".* Many believe she was referring to Shondale 'Tooka' Gregory. Tooka's friends came forward with serious threats against Young MA for disrespecting Tooka's name.

In reply to Young MA's rap, FBG Durk wrote on Twitter, *"I Ain't tryna Beef with No Female But Somebody Better Tell Her Watch Her F**king Mouth and Kno Wat She Sayin Before My Dike Cousin Bear Her."* Katorah Kasanova Marrero, also known as 'Young MA,' is an American rapper from Brooklyn.

Buff Gotti tweeted a photo of Tooka in his casket with insulting words on it. As a caption, he wrote, "LMAO. LOOK AT TOOKA." Although the tweet got many retweets, people wonder what could have led to so much hate towards Tooka.

Mocking Tooka and dancing on his grave has become commonplace in certain circles of the rap scene. Even ten years after his death, Tooka continues to pop up in lyrics and the internet.

Tooka's Brother – Lil Marc

Tooka's brother and aspiring rapper, 20-year-old Lil Marc, was killed on March 28, 2014, at a bus stop on the 300 block of East 51st Street. He released his 'No Competition,' video days before his death. In the song, he disrespected multiple deceased rival gang members. It was his little attempt at getting back at some of the rivals who had been disrespecting his dead brother, but he was doing more harm than good, and the eventual result was him paying with his life.

Marc always showed his love for Tooka on Twitter.

"Dam I miss my lil brotha i miss hearing his voice it's not a thing about u i dnt miss baby boy everyday I'm thinkn bout you #REST UP SHONDALE."

"B***h im Tooka livin proof…#GANG."

"Good morning Tooka & Fatz… #DAILYTWEETS

Antonio Davis, also known as Fatz, was shot and killed on June 22, 2012, when walking to the store with his cousin. He was just 14 years old. FBG Duck, a friend of both Tooka and Lil Marc, expressed his sadness after losing both of them, *"First I Lost My Homie Tooka Now I Just Lost The Last Thing That Look Like Him Rest Up Bro."* Carlton Weekly, also known as FBG Duck, is a Chicago rapper and member of the Fly Boy Gang (FBG), a subset of the Gangster Disciples.

Tookaville

The Gangster Disciples tagged a region of their territory, 'Tookaville,' in honor of their fallen friend, while close friends who knew Tooka formed the 'Tooka Gang.' CashOut hails from the St. Lawrence area of Chicago. He is a rapper and member of the Gangster Disciples and had a well-known beef with Chief Keef. He took Chief Keef's disses for Tooka personally and went all out to humiliate Chief Keef because Keef has infamously dissed Tooka Gang in his songs.

CashOut, who described Tooka as his 'lil homie,' spoke blatantly against the disrespect for Tooka. He says, *"One of my lil homies got killed who was like a brother to me, which is Tooka. So I'm listening and he [Chief Keef] like 'f**k Tooka Gang. I'm 3Hunna.'* Then another one of his songs he said *'f**k Tooka gang. I let this ruger bang.'"*

CashOut states how much he detests hearing those songs and what he does when they are played, *"Everytime I'm in a nice crowd of people and they play his song, everybody rocking and they say, 'f**k a Tooka gang', I done snatched a cord out somebody radio in the club once. I'm like 'man, hold up. Does anybody know Tooka? Does anybody know what he [Chief Keef] really rapping about? You can be in certain hood and riding down in Minnesota somewhere. This somebody that really died. They thinking s**t slang. No, that's a real motherf**king person who got killed."*

FBG Duck's Mother Pays Tributes to Tooka

Lasheena Weekly, Duck's mother, showed Dominique Boyd, Tooka's mother support. She experienced losing a son to gun violence and knows how it feels. Weekly visited Tooka's grave on his 10th death anniversary. She said, *"10 years baby. And guess what? You famous as f**k. Motherf*****s don't even know. The world don't even know"*.

Who's to Blame?

It's commendable to see these mothers come out to unite in grief because they share similarities in losing their children to street gang violence. On the other hand, some people believe that such unity is a little too late because it's happening after these young people have been wasted, dead, and gone. They are of the opinion that the parents should instead have rallied together to prevent these kids from belonging to the gang world. The parents should have done more to support the authorities in preventing these boys from falling into drug and criminal lifestyles.

A few other people are of the view that these parents even covered for these young people by lying and helping them to hide crimes and prevent them from being punished by the law. The parents, on their part, are blaming their ordeal on the poverty and poor education plaguing the black community and racism, especially in the dispensation of justice. They talked about how some crimes that should have ended as a slap on the wrist have ended up sentencing young men and women to serve very long prison time.

The debate is endless.

Who Is Odee Perry?

Odee Perry was born on May 13, 1991, in 10900 Block, South Racine Avenue, Chicago. Around 11:30 p.m. on Wednesday, August 10, 2011, Odee was shot multiple times, including one bullet to the neck. He was rushed to Stroger Hospital, where he was pronounced dead at 12:18 a.m. Thursday. His shooting occurred in his neighborhood near the Parkway Gardens Homes, at 64th Street, King Drive. He was just 20 years old when he died.

The young man and his family lived in an economically disadvantaged black neighborhood whose young men were involved mainly in violent gang culture. It is customary to see these young men wielding automatic rifles and pistols of all types on their social media handles. For example, Odee Perry has multiple Twitter posts with different guns, from regular firearms to automatic rifles.

The young rapper is well "repped" and honored in his 'hood.' He even appeared in Chief Keef's music videos wielding various guns. Other rappers who have made songs in his honor include Lil Reese, King Von, Lil Durk, and Booka 600. Odee is a ladies' man as he is often seen in the company of women in pictures.

Shooting

Odee was said to be a cool guy who loved hanging out with his friends. He helped the Black Disciples fight for Parkway Gardens, transforming it from a harbor of the Gangster Disciples to a Black Disciples territory. He achieved this along with other WIIC (wild, insane, and crazy) city members like Boss-Top, J-money, E-Dog, and BJ.

Who Killed Odee Perry?

Odee's killers remain unknown and never apprehended; however, top on the list of suspected persons responsible is Gakirah Barnes, aka K.I, a friend of Tooka. The infamous Gangster Disciple member who had previously boasted of killing 17 people was never charged with Odee's murder; however, people thought she was the one who pulled the trigger, and the suspicion remained for three years. With more than 5,000 Twitter followers, Gakirah was the most notorious shooter in the neighborhood's history.

However, it was a matter of pride for gangs to claim responsibility for shootings and murders and some other sects and individuals claimed responsibility for Odee's death. For example, one member of a different gang, with a Twitter handle "FatzGeng Marc Bloc," made a post on Twitter saying, "We made Oblock, we left yo man on a poster." One Rugo, Mobscrap's brother, has lyrics in his song that said, "Nigga talk that sh**t, but they don't even know who made the O."

Odee Perry, The Legend of O Block

The Parkway Gardens development is a low-income, privately-owned apartment complex sitting on one side of the road. In contrast, on the other side, you will see a string of businesses like a food mart, the Chicago Crusader newspaper, and an Auto Zone. On the map, it is the 6400 block of South Dr. Martin Luther King Jr. Drive. This is the most dangerous block in Chicago and America and got it's nickname from Odee who was only one of 19 people shot on O Block between 2011 and 2014.

On a typical day in O Block, you will see young men in hoodies and sagged jeans gather in groups smoking marijuana. They stare at strangers while parents hold tight to their young ones as they travel between the neighborhood school, business place, and the safety of their apartments. On O Block, you never know when violence will erupt between rival street gangs.

It was also home to the former US First Lady, Michelle Obama. Her family moved away from Parkway gardens before she was 2. At that time, Parkway Gardens was an innovative Black-owned cooperative. A once family-focused environment turned out to be a place a lot of people fear.

Words on the Street About Odee:

Fredo Santana, a member of the Black Disciples and Chief Keef's older cousin, paid tribute to Odee in Gang bang. He said *"BANG BANG like Chief Keef, R.I.P to Odee!"*

Carlton D. Weekly (FBG Duck) released a music video called 'Dead Bitches'. In a part of the video, he mentions a rival gang member, Odee Perry. He says, *"Said I wasn't gon' diss the dead and okay, I did it. But n...., f... T-Roy and Odee, them dead bitches."*

In an interview with King Von, he says, *"O'Block is really OD (Odee Perry), which was my homie who passed away. That was my brother."*

Gakirah Barnes, aka KI/Lil Snoop – The Lady Assassin

Gakirah Barnes is known as the most notorious female gang assassin in Chicago and one of the most infamous female gang assassins in American history. Her alias 'K.I.' was from her name, while she was also called 'Lil Snoop' after a female gang assassin in the movie, 'The Wire.' The shy, gap-toothed young girl turned into a killer with a reckless thirst for revenge. Unfortunately, she died exactly the way she lived her life, by the gun. At the young age of 17, she was gunned down and added to the ever-growing list of Chicago young lives that never make it to age 20 due to their gang affiliations and criminal lifestyles.

Her Early Years

Gakirah was born in January 1997 on the Southside of Chicago. She was raised in 63rd St Lawrence to another struggling Black Chicago family who happened to be surrounded by members of the Gangster Disciples and plagued with gang-related crimes and violence. An aunt had this to say about K.I, *"I lived with her mother, who described her as a sweet loving girl, though she admitted she was not particularly an angel."* As a promising student in her early teens, K.I. wanted to become a social worker to help those who tend to get lost in the system, but her priorities changed as she got involved with the gang life.

K.I was a gifted young lady. She attended the perspectives/IIT Math and Science Academy, and in her eighth grade, she entered the South Side Charter school, where she was suspended for being disrespectful in her first month. According to her assistant principal, Gakirah was a shy kid, but she became less guarded and made friends as the year progressed. However, when she entered her freshman year, her attendance declined, and she would later drop out after she landed in the juvenile justice system.

As one who grew up in the South Side of Chicago, it would only be natural to find her hanging out with street boys, especially the St Lawrence boys, as a teenager. She started attending their parties, and at 14, she was charged with firing a gun, but the eyewitness later recanted for fear of retaliation or reprisal attacks, so the case was dismissed.

Some people believed watching her friends get shot and killed probably fueled K.I.'s desire for the respect and protection a gang membership would provide. On the other hand, other people concluded that based on the neighborhood where she grew up, it was only natural that even though she was a girl, she would end up a criminal gang member just as she did. Gakirah's record with the authorities multiplied as she grew older.

Her father was murdered on Easter Sunday in 1997 when she was less than a year old. She is survived by her mother, Shantell Brown, two older brothers, a younger brother, and a younger sister.

Gang Affiliation

Gakirah was associated with the Fly Boy Gang and she belonged to the STL, a set of Gangster Disciples located on 63rd St Lawrence and 64th Eberhart. They had issues with O'Block, 600, and other gangs. Gakirah was affiliated with other notable figures like FBG Young, Wooksi, Dutchie, Lil Jay, FBG Duck, and FBG Butta.

Gakirah's life changed at 13 when her friend, Shondale' Tooka' Gregory, was shot and killed. Gakirah changed her Facebook name to 'Tookaville Kirah' after the incident. Tooka's killers mocking him on social media and in their rap songs turned Gakirah's grief and that of her fellow gang members to rage.

Later that year, about eight months after Tooka's death, Odee Perry, was gunned down. Gakirah was suspected of having killed Odee as a way of avenging Tooka's death, but she was never charged with the murder due to lack of evidence.

However, K.I. boasted on her Twitter handle, suggesting she shot and killed Odee Perry. There were photo images of her showing off Odee's firearm on her Twitter handle while mocking his death, suggesting that she must have been present at Odee's shooting. Some of these photos have since been taken down but that was after thousands of followers had seen them and formed their opinion. Lastly, Odee's shooting and murder took place on Tooka's birthday.

Gakirah lost another member of her gang, 17-year-old Carlton 'Tutu' Archer, in November 2011. He was found dead in an alley after being shot in the West Woodlawn neighborhood. She put up a photo of him with the caption, '*RIP Carlton*'.

On June 24, 2012, Gakirah's cousin, 13-year-old Tyquan Tyler, was murdered. They were close enough that Gakirah referred to him as her little brother. Tyquan's mother moved him to West Illinois to get him away from violence. Tyquan had come to visit Gakirah from outside the city. He begged his mother to let him attend a party with Gakirah. Unfortunately, he would be at the wrong place at the wrong time.

While they were leaving the party on the 6200 block of South Rhodes Avenue, two men started firing into the crowd, and a stray bullet hit Tyquan in the chest. The men were identified as Jiro City members Nasean Flowers and Dewayne Chester. They were fighting with members of the St. Lawrence Boys gang when Tyquan was shot.

Tyquan's mother, Sandra Tyler, was on her way to pick him up when the incident happened. She said, '*I held him in my hands while he was fighting for his life.*' Some hours later, he was declared dead in a children's hospital. Gakirah's friend said she had never seen a hardened gangster cry like Gakirah did that night.

After such a heartbreaking experience, Gakirah tweeted, '*Tyquan supposed 2 Be hear wit me But instead Lil Bro ended up 6 feet under a million miles away.*' From the day Tyquan died, she dedicated herself to his revenge, calling herself, TyquanAssassin.

Gakirah's 17-year-old cousin, Rodney Stewart, also known as 'Boss Trell,' was shot and killed on November 12, 2012. He was a member of the Gangster Disciples from St. Lawrence and was about to move to Iowa to live with his two friends two days before he was shot. There were rumors that his murder was a case of revenge by rival gangs. He was shot in the head in an alley near the 2600 block of 83rd street. Boss Trell is praised by members of his gang like Cashout in their rap songs.

It seemed like Gakirah's grief would never end, when on March 28, 2014, another tragedy happened when a 19-year-old Reason 'Lil B' Shaw, a member of the Gangster Disciples, was killed by the Chicago police. He was accused of participating in a drug transaction. After the Police approached him, he fled the scene, leaving them on a foot chase. Police said that while between two buildings in the Woodlawn neighborhood, he pointed a handgun at them and, they had to open fire. He was shot seven times.

Over 100 onlookers gathered and protested that Lil B never had a weapon. Gakirah tweeted, '*Da pain unbearable.*' She posted again, '*Police took my homie I dedicate my life 2 his revenge 100*'. She also sent the Police a warning tweet, '*DA Police I'd kill u Faster Dan n****z on Da Corner.*' Gakirah was said to keep a stack of newspaper stories about her friends slain in street violence.

On April 9, Chief Keef's 30-year-old cousin, member of the Black Disciples and father of five, Mario 'Blood Money' Hess, was shot dead just weeks after signing a record contract with Interscope Records. He was a Drill rapper and killed on the 5600 block of South Elizabeth Street in Englewood. Gakirah posted on Twitter the next day,' *u Nobody until Somebody kill u dats jst real Shyt.*'

The murder of Blood Money got a lot of attention, and rumors spread that Gakirah was the killer. Police suspected Gakirah but did not charge her with the murder. It was said that Blood Money's gang members were out for revenge. Later, Lil Jay, a fellow Gang member of Gakirah, posted a video of him drinking a red-colored liquid, singing *'Sippin' on Blood Money.'* The video aroused more suspicion.

Gakirah continued to express her grief online by renaming her Twitter Profile *'No surrender Lil B.'* On April 10, she tweeted, *'I Dne seen 2 many of my n****z n a casket…In da end we DIE'*. It was almost as if she knew her time was up.

The Death of K.I.

Two days after the slaying of Blood Money, Winooski, a Gangster Disciple, tweeted at Gakirah, wondering where she was. She responded, *"On my way 2 Da Land WAY."*

Winooski responded, *"On my way to the block."*

Gakirah dressed and got ready to leave the house. She tweeted *'6347 TMB'*, which was suspected to be a hangout spot for the STL/EBT. She was believed to be walking to that address to hang out with her friends when she was shot in the 6400 block of South Eberhart Avenue. This event happened at about 3:30 pm on Friday, April 11, 2014, which was her cousin's Boss Trell's birthday. Two other people were also shot on that day.

Eyewitness accounts state that an unknown figure wearing a grey hoodie and blue jeans approached the three victims with a handgun and began firing. Nine shots were fatally fired to Gakirah's chest, neck, and jaw, leaving her bleeding on the pavement. Afterward, the shooter escaped into an unknown vehicle. She managed to crawl to the steps of a house nearby, where she eventually lost consciousness. Gakirah was pronounced dead two hours later at Northwestern Memorial Hospital. She was buried close to her father.

Police were said to have reacted to about 27 incidents in the West Woodlawn area when Gakirah was killed. Four people were killed. The temperature of Chicago was also reported to have soared into the 80s, making that time the hottest year in 2014. Some people suspect that the increased temperature could have played a role in the shootings that weekend.

Prior to her death, some policemen made some effort to save Gakirah from the streets. Two police officers visited a male gang member to warn him to stay away from guns or go to prison. While on this mission, they spotted Gakirah in the alley of 63rd Street near King Drive, the border of the Black Disciples. She risked getting killed there, so the policemen got out of their car to offer her help. She refused and walked away, and in less than two months, she was killed. It was suspected that Gakirah went there looking for D. Rose, who uploaded a video insulting Lil B.

For several years, the police have been investigating the death of Gakirah. Dayvon Bennett, also known as 'King Von,' was named as Gakirah's killer. This is partly due to his controversial lyrics like '*I swear I killed her, broke her back,*' from the "Expose Me" remix. He also said, '*put a pretty opp b***h in a morgue, huh. Call that b***h drop dead gorgeous, damn*'. However, there wasn't enough evidence so charges were never filed against him.

King Von was charged with first-degree murder, when he shot and killed 19-year-old college student Malcolm Stuckey on May 29, 2014. He was arrested on July 24, 2014, but after witnesses failed to testify in 2017, all charges were dropped. The Chicago Police Department released new information naming King Von as Gakirah's killer. Witnesses also reported seeing the late rapper hoodied up before allegedly killing Gakirah.

Gakirah's Rap Sheet

Gakirah was alleged to have killed more than a dozen people by the time of her death. Many say she might have been responsible for up to 20 murders, while some claimed she caught her first body as early as age 14. She posted pictures and videos of herself with guns and making threats against rival gangs. Though Gakirah had been arrested numerous times, she had never been arrested for any crime close to murder.

K.I. is suspected of being involved in multiple gang slayings, but the two most talked-about are the killing of Odee Perry and Blood Money. She put up some tweets mocking Odee after his death. They include, '*s/o to odee for bein target practice lol,*' '*rolling up da dope I fanna odee*' among other insulting tweets.

She also tweeted about 21-year-old JMoney, who was shot in the head. '*Shoot a Nigga Frm Point blank Range n Da Back of Da Head*' ending the tweet with a gun and devil emoji. '*JMoney Aint use his head So we Took It Off.*' She loved mocking the death of fallen members of the opposing gang, and she was aggressive during heated gang exchanges.

K.I. appeared in a Fly Boy Gang music video by FBG Young and FBG Dutchie titled Murda, where she was seen tying a bandana covering her face and pointing an automatic gun at the camera. A line, 'K.I. my young killa,' was used to refer to her. The Fly Boy Gang wanted to get the attention of music producers who had taken an interest in street raps performed by people who were actually 'living' their songs.

Over time, Gakirah got so good at shooting that she learned never to get caught. Her name and reputation also got more attention from the authorities, and she gained respect on the streets..

Words on The Street About K.I.

Mother of Gakirah, Shantell Brown, called the situation in Chicago '*an ongoing war*'. She added '*This is something that has become all too normal to everybody, and it needs to stop. Like we need to come together as a community and just unite to get our children and our street back*'. Brown also stated that she was in control of her daughter when she was at home, but on the street, she thinks Gakirah became another person. In her words, '*I guess she felt, I can't be the good girl my mom wants me to be – I have to be a badass.*' She says her daughter is not the person she is being portrayed to be.

Gakirah's Twitter account is filled with tributes. *They killed my little ni**a snoop #restuptyquanassassin*', a member of the Fly Boy Gang tweeted. Lil Jay posted a picture of Gakirah pointing her hand like a gun with the caption, 'Rip K I Da Shooter.'

The battle continued in the comment section. On April 15, four days after Gakirah's death, 16-year-old Keno Glass, an aspiring rapper and cousin of Lil Jojo, was shot dead. Her death is also being mocked online, chiefly by rival gang members. Blogs and different social networks are filled with stories of Gakirah, letting out varying rumors and truths about her life.

Gakirah has even become immortalized through various social media platforms. Many people are fascinated with her stories. To STL/EBT, she will always be their little sister, and to her mother, she will be a loving daughter, and to the gang world, K.I. will always be remembered as a fearless and ruthless shooter.

The Stats Keeping Piling Up

Gakirah's death is another addition to the cruel statistic from a city struggling with gun violence. Gunshot injury was found to be the third leading cause of death among children aged 17 and younger. 1,300 minors die from shootings each year in the United States, and 5,800 are injured. The death rate of African American children is ten times higher than for white/Asian Americans. Almost half of the young black people were said to have experienced a gang-related killing. Social media increases gun violence as fights start on social media with insults and move to the street as violence. Gakirah's dark social media presence is now used to help crime fighters detect possible violence on social media. They use artificial intelligence to make early interventions before matters get out of hand. Social media violence is now known as Cyber ganging with today's teens.

Female shooters in gangs are not typical, but K.I.'s reputation has increased female involvement. Girls are becoming more and more involved in violence, but usually with their hands and fists and not with firearms. There are only a few cases of girls pulling the trigger during gang shootings, and Gakirah's case was one of them. Many factors, her friend's death being number one, played a significant role in shaping the kind of life Gakirah lived.

Chapter Ten

Dayvon Daquan Bennett, aka King Von/Grandson – A True King of the Street

King Von will always be remembered for his street storytelling, love for his homeland, and close relationship with Lil Durk. These say a lot about him, but his story has just begun.

Who is King Von?

Dayvon Daquan Bennett, also known as 'King Von', was born on August 9, 1994, to Taesha and Walter Bennett. He grew up east of Englewood and the Dan Ryan Expressway in Parkway Gardens, also known as 'O Block.' He had six half-siblings from his father and three from his mother. His siblings include Kayla B., Yung Bogo, Sky, and Louie V.

As a result of his dad being in and out of jail, Von was raised mainly by his mother. His father was allegedly shot and killed by a rival gang when Von was just 11. He ended up spending only three years with his dad, as they first met when he was 8.

Von dedicated a post on his Instagram profile to his dad:

"Men this due right here is the definition of #Real. He taught me so much when it came to the street s**t choosing your circle wisely and most of all #loyalty. #SILK ADA PARK FINEST… When it comes to being a real loyal standup N**** it was him I miss you Homie and the streets an most definitely your kids do too… Chicago haven't been the same since you left and it would never be the same."

In one of his songs, Von said he wishes his family was closer. In an interview, he said, "*My family was close before my grandma passed away not too long ago. We used to all meet up over at her house. She kept everybody close. Time goes by and s**t just changes, man. People get old. People got their own s**t going on.*"

The Name 'Grandson'

One of King Von's nicknames is 'Grandson.' In a 2018 interview, Von joked that he earned the nickname 'Grandson' because he's related to David Barksdale. He explained:

"When I was in jail, I got the name Grandson because I reminded people of King David. The older guys in jail, guys who were around when David was around, would call me that 'cause I carried myself like him. King David was a legendary figure and a guy everybody looked up to. He ran the streets with his own morals and his own code, and that's the code I live by too. That's why people call me Grandson."

King Von always wore an 'O Block' chain from Icebox, showing his love and loyalty to the Black Disciples and his close-knit relationship with his late buddy Odee Perry.

Why Atlanta?

King Von said he left Chicago for Atlanta to find peace and escape the trouble in his hometown. He did not want to stay in Chicago because the police and rival gang members were too familiar with his moves. In an interview, he stated, *"I love Atlanta because I live there with no problems and s**t, and that's where there are more rappers. I like Chicago better though because I have my people there, but the Police know me there too well in Chicago and there are people that don't like me."*

Von's Rap Sheet

King Von frequently got into trouble with the police in Chicago and was sent to jail for the first time in November 2012, when he was only 16 years old. He was arrested and booked into Cook County jail for possessing a firearm unlawfully.

On July 24, 2014, King Von and Michael Wade allegedly opened fire during a birthday party in Englewood, leading to the death of Malcolm Stuckey; two other men were wounded. Von was charged with one charge of murder and two counts of attempted murder. Michael Wade was given a 28-year sentence for aggravated battery. In 2017, Von was found 'not guilty' after witnesses failed to testify.

King Von was also arrested in 2018 after the police raided an apartment in Parkway Gardens where they found a suitcase containing handguns and marijuana. Cook County prosecutors failed to file charges against him because they did not have enough to put him away.

In June 2019, about a year after King Von moved to Atlanta, he was arrested alongside Lil Durk in connection with a shooting in Atlanta. Both men allegedly shot a man outside Atlanta's popular Varsity hotdog stand and stole $30,000 worth of jewelry and a vehicle. The shooting took place in February 2019. After weeks in jail, they were released on bond and placed on electronic monitoring, but the case remained open.

During the bail hearing, an Atlanta police officer testified that a surveillance camera caught Lil Durk shooting at the victim. A Chicago police detective also traveled to Atlanta and testified that both rappers were active members of the Black Disciples. According to law enforcement sources, the Black Disciples were known for trafficking guns and marijuana in Atlanta.

In July 2021, Chicago police received new information concerning the death of 17-year-old Gakirah 'K.I.' Barnes. Investigations revealed that Dayvon 'King Von' Bennett was the hooded figure that fired the multiple shots that killed Gakirah Barnes.

In a 2019 interview with a podcast, King Von said he found it easier to do time in jail in Atlanta than in Cook County, where rivals would pick fights with him. In Atlanta, he said inmates would approach him because they were fans of his music.

The King's Music Career

King Von started doing rap songs when he was in jail on a murder charge. He taught himself to rap without a beat. His breakout single was 'Crazy Story' which was released on December 6, after Lil Durk signed Von to his Only the Family (OTF) label. Lil Durk took Von under his wing and helped mold him as an artist.

Many of King Von's popular songs pay tribute to Chicago, and he was best known as the 'Chronicler of the Street Life.' He talks about the stress, poverty, trauma, and pain of growing up in Chicago.

On Valentine's Day of 2019, Von's girlfriend, Asian Doll, released the music video of 'Grandson,' a track about Von in which he appeared. In the same year, Von released 'Crazy Story 2' featuring Lil Durk. A while later, he released 'Crazy Story 3'. Von talks about everything that made him a famous rapper in 'Crazy Story,' one of his biggest hits.

In July 2019, Von collaborated with Lil Durk and released, 'Like That.' In September of the same year, Von dropped his single, 'What's it Like.' In the same month, he released his 15-track mixtape, 'Grandson Vol. 1'. The album debuted at number 75 on the Billboard 200 and number 27 on the HipHop/R&B Albums chart.

November 2019 saw the release of '2 am' and 'Rolling' featuring YNW Melly. In 2020, the rapper did not slow down despite the pandemic and received success with additional tracks. He released

'Pressin', 'Took Her to the O,' and a mixtape, 'Levon James,' which became number 63 on the Billboard 200. About a week before Von's death, he released an album, 'Welcome to O Block.'

In an interview with Audiomack, King Von was asked what he wanted his latest album, 'Welcome to O Block' to teach others. He replied:

"I don't know what it's going to teach them, but what you're going to get out of that s**t is some real savage street s**t. It's going to tell you about a lot of street s**t, s**t that n****s that'll be in the hood a lot go through."

The former manager of King Von said that Von was a workaholic who had two albums worth of unreleased music. One of his music videos, 'Demon', completed about a month before his death, was released posthumously. King Von worked so hard to stamp his name in the hearts of many. It was as though he knew he would not live long.

The Death of the King

Friday, November 6, 2020, would be the day that King Von's life would be terminated by what may have seemed insignificant.

One week after he released his album, 'Welcome to O Block," along with a group of men, King Von was said to have left the Opium nightclub for Monaco Hookah Lounge on Trinity Avenue. A dispute ensued between two groups of men in the parking lot of the Lounge. King Von was reportedly involved in an argument with another rapper, Tyquain Terrel Bowman, popularly known as 'Quando Rondo.' The dispute escalated to gunfire. One off-duty police officer and one on-duty officer on patrol intervened to stop the shootings. The shootings were said to have happened around 2:15 am.

The 26-year-old King Von was taken to Grady Hospital in Atlanta by a private vehicle in critical condition, where he died later that day.

The Georgia Bureau of Investigation reported that three people were killed and three wounded after the shooting.

Surveillance footage shows a group of men in the parking lot of the Hookah Lounge before King Von aggressively approaches Quando and begins punching him in the head. Seconds later, shots were fired, and the men were seen scattering and taking cover.

One of those wounded was the suspect in the killing of King Von, 22-year-old Timothy 'Lil Tim' Leeks. He was placed in police custody while being treated at Grady Hospital for a gunshot wound. The Savannah native was released from Fulton County jail after a $100,000 bond was posted on March 20, 2021.

Leeks graduated from Jenkins High School in 2016. The Savannah Police Department arrested Leeks in 2020. He was charged with attempting to violate the Georgia Controlled Substance Act, theft by receiving stolen property, and obstruction after an investigation that led to the seizure of marijuana and $16,000. Also, 34-year-old Mark Blakely, a member of the Black Disciples, was one of the three people killed in the shooting. He was a felon with gun and theft convictions in Cook County.

There were rumors that an Atlanta police officer who came to intervene in the shootings shot King Von, but the police claimed he was shot during the initial shootout before the police intervened in an attempt to stop the shooting.

Quando Rondo released a record titled, 'End of Story' where he talks about his involvement in King Von's fatal shooting. He recalled the incident while referring to the surveillance footage showing King Von assaulting Quando before the shooting started. He raps:

"Blood on your brother, on the ground, gon' pick your mans up

Damn right we screaming self-defense

He shouldn't have never put his hands on me

Look at the footage, that's all the evidence

See them p**** n****'s shouldn't have ran up on me

Who the f*** said I was hidin'?

I'm still ridin' round with them bands on me

And to set records straight, I ain't never had no show inside the A."

Quando Rondo was insulted on Twitter for trying to justify Von's death.

King Von was buried in a private ceremony on November 15, 2020, in Chicago. The location was kept secret.

The Aftermath of the King's Passing

King Von's death started as a rumor on Twitter before it was confirmed by those close to him. A flood of tributes followed.

Chopsquad DJ, who produced beats for King Von, took to Instagram to share his tribute:

"My heart can't take this. No bro. Why you. Why bro. Please just Facetime me bro. Why they had to take you. Ima see you again this s***t ain't over. It's far from over. We still just getting started. RIP my best friend. The only n**** to listen to me word for word from day 1. We sat on Facetime for hours making songs together. Every bar had a meaning and every song was a part of our soul. Every moment meant something and to grow wit you made me feel like I was a real producer. I love you bro @kingvonfrmdao"

King Von's publicist, Eric Ryan, shared:

"Dayvon Bennett emerged from difficult circumstances to become one of music's most promising stars. The 26-year-old artist left us as the world

was beginning to grasp the depths of his talents. He overcame myriad unjust circumstances yet remained steadfastly dedicated to giving back to the community that raised him 'O' Block'."

Fellow rapper and collaborator to King Von, Chance the Rapper, posted: *"Wow. This year was so tough, RIP Von God bless him and his family I can't believe it. Was a real one 100 & a good hearted n****."*

Calboy posted, *'No, not Cuzo!* (heartbreak emoji).

Omarion paid tribute: *"Rest in Power, Von. I seen the potential. I heard a few songs but more than I seen him breaking bread with his family. I respect that. I connect with that."*

After Von's death, Von's close friend, Asian Doll, tweeted: *'I wanna die 2. Shid, it feels like I died already.'* In a now-deleted tweet, she claimed King Von used his last breath to blame his friends for his murder:

"Von's last words 'y'all let them n****s get up on me'. Stop crying y'all let them get me. Y'all left my boy when he was unarmed & he would've hawked mfs down for them & spent AGAIN & AGAIN & AGAIN s**t crazy I knew my boy HEART & LOYALTY wasn't deserved he OK tho."

King Von's manager, Track, responded to Asian Doll and others who made speculations about the Rapper's death. He wrote on his Instagram story:

"Let one more person from the outside that's close to Von keep on with all this goffy s**t. I promise I'm a expose all that goffy s**t, 'cause I was there n got shot behind this. Y'all stop blaming people y'all don't even know what happen or who was involved. Y'all see one camera angle and think y'all figured it out. That goes for girlfriend, family or whoever."

Canadian R&B duo Daniel Daley and Nineteen85, collectively known as dsvn, expressed their condolences:

"In a time where there's so much divide we really gotta get this into the right perspective... we're not the enemy... we have to do better now... Rest in power King Von."

Also, K. Michelle, a fan of King Von's music, took to Instagram to praise the rapper and ask that the tragic killing be stopped. She wrote:

"I'm honestly tired of us getting killed. Anybody that knows me knows how much I loved some @kingvonfrmdao. I don't listen to a lot of rap, but I listened to him and his storytelling daily. This really hit me hard this morning. Dear God bless his sister, his kids, his whole family. I cant believe this. Why every day another young talent has to be takin from us? He left behind fans that adore him, me being one. RIP @kingvonfrmdao Stop this dumb a** killing."

One of King Von's baby mamas, Kema, said King Von had *'prepped me for this* and *'coached on what to do if this happened.'* She said:

'Von, baby I'm so lost. I'm so sorry we always get into it and say things we don't mean, get back cool and laugh at it. You know my heart, you know I'll protect you and my son forever... we just talked and you told me everything was going to get better... You made it, you beat the odd. Your secrets are safe with me.'

Lil Durk, a very close friend of King Von, took to Instagram to pay his tribute: *"MY TWIN GONE. I LOVE YOU BABY BRO D-ROY!!!!"* He posted this alongside a picture of Von. Lil Durk also customized jackets with the King Von portrait on them. During one of his performances, he flashed a white suede jacket that had a large portrait of King Von. Lil Durk also has a hat collection with the words' V-Roy' on the side. He posted on Instagram, saying, *"All hats should say V. roy or you can't wear em around us."*

After King Von's death, Lil Durk used Von's O Block chain in his music video, 'Backdoor' to pay tribute to his late friend and collaborator. King Von also posthumously appeared on Lil Durk's voice trap, 'Still Trappin'.

King Von posthumously received his Billboard Hot 100 hits in November 2020 with four different titles: 'Took Her to the O,' 'The Code,' feat. Polo G, 'All These N***as,' feat. Lil Durk, and 'Crazy Story 2.0,' feat. Lil Durk. The songs mark the first time he made the ranking.

During the 63rd annual Grammy Awards, King Von was included in the Memoriam montage. An artist also painted a mural of King Von across the street from O Block. The mural caught public attention on what would have been Von's 27th birthday. Police asked the artist to remove the mural a week later. However, before its removal, Lil Durk visited the street art to pay tribute to his friend, King Von.

6ix9ine, in reply to Lil Durk visiting King Von's mural, stated:

"Lil Tim put that man on on a Damn Wall smh... he's been on several T-shirts .. hats... he's just a Diamond chain now... he really said 'if I was to die my ni***** gon slide every day.....'" Lil Tim is the street name of Von's suspected killer, Timothy Leeks.

Daniel Hernandez, also known as 6ix9ine, is an American rapper known for his aggressive rapping style. After Von's death, 6ix9ine consistently looked for an opportunity to mock the late rapper. Once, a post was shared by a close friend of 6ix9ine suggesting that Lil Durk learned about King Von's death on Instagram Live. 6ix9ine replied in the comments with a laughing emoji. He also commented on another post about King Von, saying, *"King Von is burning in hell and I'm here for it."*

6ix9ine, who has been having disputes with Chicago-based rappers, shared two photos on Instagram with the caption, *"F A N**** KILLLA AINT DEAD YOU SHOULDN'T WEAR NO RIP SHIRTS."* In the first photo, he wore a King Von shirt, and in the next, he was lying on the floor playing dead.

King Von is survived by two kids, a baby mama, a pregnant girlfriend, and other siblings. Kema shared a photo showing Von's kids standing by his coffin. They cried as it descended into the ground. King Von's sister, Kayla B, also confirmed that the rapper has another child with a woman named Skyler Knight on the way. This will make King Von a father of three – two girls and a boy. She shared pictures and videos of the baby shower on Twitter. She tweeted on June 2021.

'Today von baby mama baby shower wish he was here 2 be with us We gone make sure she str8 tho!"

Luckily for King Von's children, their father owned the royalties to his music, ensuring that his two children were financially secure for a long time.

Philanthropic Gestures

The founder of Mothers/Men Against Senseless Killings (MASK), Tama Manasseh, took to social media, recalling the first time she met Von. She said that on Christmas day, 2019, she and other volunteers were in Parkway Gardens during their 'Sleigh ride,' when Von pulled up to the group, asking how he could help. He said, '*I don't have any gifts on me, but can I pass out these dollars to the kids?*' Occasionally, King Von went to his Parkway Garden neighborhood with money and gave it to families and children in need.

She explained, "*I was just proud of a kid who could've done anything with that money and could've been anywhere doing it, but chose to be there with us on Christmas morning, giving. Before he left, he smiled and told me, 'I wish somebody would've did this for [him and other young men in his entourage] when we were shortys.'*"

Manasseh said she saw humanity in him and not King Von. She saw a kid on Christmas morning giving gifts to other kids. She couldn't understand how he could be the person murdered in Atlanta.

Chapter Eleven

Ameer Golston, aka Aab Hellabandz – A Short Time Celebrity Status

Ameer Golston was a fast-rising Chicago-born Drill celebrity rapper who was shot and killed at the age of 24-years old. Ameer rose to popularity with his hit tracks, "Hellabandz," and "Count Wrong."

Aab Hellabandz, as he was popularly known, was born in Chicago, Illinois, on January 5, 1995. He gained public attention with his music in 2016 when he released his hit singles "Hatn," and "Hellabandz." Like several Drill artists, Ameer has a couple of songs under his name and collaborations with other artists. Again, the standard features in these music videos are the same. For example, in one of his singles, "Mad," you hear lovely music playing with young men in dreads smoking weeds and other hard drugs wielding automatic firearms back and forth.

Other songs and collaborations by Ameer Golson, aka Aab Hellabandz, include, "Pick A Door," "Got Da Strap," "Trap, Smoke, & Sip Drink," and many more. Ameer is notorious for showing off guns, cash, drugs, and tattoos in his songs. Ameer's celebrity status rose a notch when pictures of him and Blac Chyna started showing up on his social media handles. There were even rumors of a relationship between the duo.

The Chicago-based rapper is ranked as one of the most popular rappers from that part of the country, with his net worth said to be valued at millions of dollars.

Crime and Death

Like hundreds and thousands of young Drill rappers from Chicago who are wasting away in various jails or buried below due to gang affiliation and criminal lifestyle, Ameer Golson suffered his fate on May 11, 2019, in the full view of the world.

There were three separate, unconnected shootings on that fateful night in Miami, Florida. The first was outside a crowded South Florida Beachfront hotel, the second shooting was on a busy Miami Beach street, while the third was on a major highway, although with no severe injuries. It was a busy day for the authorities having to deal with these different issues in one night.

The major event that night was the all-involved hip-hop performers and guests of the Rolling Loud Festival. It was a three-day event that started on Friday night to be wrapped up spectacularly on Sunday night. The venue of the event was the Miami Dolphins Stadium. After an extensive investigation of trying to confirm the connection between the three incidents, police authorities later confirmed that each incident stood alone.

In a press conference on the events of that night, a spokesman for the Miami Beach police, Ernesto Rodriguez, said, *"It is all something we are investigating, but it is too early to tell."* The organizers of the event later posted on their Twitter handle saying, *"IF YOU DIDN'T ENJOY ROLLING LOUD DESPITE THE HICCUPS, STAY HOME NEXT YEAR… THIS IS HIP-HOP."* That account was later suspended for being insensitive to the various events that happened that night, especially the ones that affected the event and led to the loss of lives.

One of the most notable shootings of that weekend took place 36 hours before that of Ameer's. Shooters in a drive-by Cadillac Escalade opened fire on rapper NBA YoungBoy and his entourage as they were coming out of the Trump International Beach Resort Miami. Fortunately, no life was lost, but the rapper's girlfriend, Kyalyn Marie

Long, was injured, and a stray bullet grazed another 5-year-old bystander.

Members of the YoungBoy's entourage who were legally allowed to carry firearms returned fire, and one of their bullets hit another 43-year-old bystander, Mohamed Jradi, right in his van on the other side of the street. The police did not charge any member of the YoungBoy's entourage or the rapper himself because they returned fire in self-defense.

According to police official records, 26-year-old Hall Austin is responsible for the violent shooting and murder of Ameer Golston who was gunned down in the middle of the street.

Austin Hall, who had just been convicted of armed robbery, had a few days to go before he presented himself to prison authorities to start serving his time. He traveled to Miami to settle an old score with Ameer. Like Hall, Ameer was also known to authorities as a suspect in a previous murder case that involved a shooting. This was said about the South Beach shooting of Ameer, *"It was pretty brazen to assassinate somebody in the middle of the street, next to a nightclub that was packed."*

It was about 2:40 a.m. on May 11, 2019, when multiple gunshots were fired. Several people could tell it was coming from the Washington Avenue area of Espanola Way. The gunshots sent people fleeing and scampering for safety. The police would later find Ameer Golston lying unresponsive and motionless on his left side around 200 Block of Espanola Way. The police immediately identified Ameer by the State of Arizona ID card he had on him.

About two hours earlier, Ameer Golston, who was not scheduled to perform that night, can be seen through surveillance cameras arriving at the venue. Later that night, he was seen on video in the company of several people walking east on Espanola Way. Not long after that time, Austin Hall was seen as he arrived at the Cameo Night Club in the company of two other men. Hall was pictured talking on his cell phone while walking a few steps behind Ameer and his company. However, it was not until Ameer got to the bend of Espanola Way and Washington Avenue that Hall and his friend walked past them.

Eyewitnesses confirmed that Hall stepped in front of Ameer, and both men started exchanging words before Hall punched Ameer. The latter could be seen in the surveillance footage as he staggered backward from the weight of the punch. He then turns to run away from Hall as he is also defending himself. Hall raised his hands with his gun fully loaded and started firing at Ameer as he turned to run away. The Drill rapper tried to avoid being hit by running in between cars, but he fell face to the ground as Hall caught up with him after a short chase.

The police report and onlookers said Hall stood over Ameer's lifeless body face-down and fired several shots, hitting him in the back and on his head before running off. Another injured victim was found not far from Ameer and was taken to Ryder Trauma Hospital to treat his non-life-threatening injury.

The Chicago Police Department identified Hall as the same person arrested in 2017 for possessing a stolen vehicle and using a firearm by a convicted felon.

For his part, Ameer was said to be involved in a shooting that killed an affiliate of Austin Hall. The latter tracked Ameer to that event to exert revenge.

One bystander described the whole shooting this way, *"I was just walking by, and I heard gunshots," "It was just ... It's crazy. This town is going nuts."*

Here's what the police spokesman said about the shooting, *"It was wanted out of Atlanta PD, actually, he had an active warrant for attempted murder. Lots of folks there. Thankfully, no one else was wounded."*

You Live by The Sword and Die by The Sword

In a legal deposition, the police identified the Chicago-based Drill rapper Ameer Golston as the alleged shooter of one Christopher Hooper in March 2015 at the notorious Adrianna's nightclub. Hooper was an aspiring rapper from Matteson, who was at the club for a performance by rap artist Future on the night he was shot and killed by Ameer.

While the Markham Police refused any further comment on the status of the investigation into the shooting and murder of Christopher Hooper, the latter's aunt, Jennel Hooper, said, *"it's a closure for us."* The Cook County State's Attorney's office too refused to say anything about the status of the case despite all inquiries. Despite the revelation and legal deposition, the Golston family has remained silent over the matter.

Adrianna, the nightclub where Ameer had allegedly shot and killed Christopher Hooper, has had its fair share of a long history of violence, especially between Christmas Eve of 2010 and July 2016, with eight people fatally shot. The club was renamed Stadium Plus in 2016 under the management of new owners; it would later close down a few months after police shot a man outside the club, claiming he had threatened them with his firearm.

Despite several outbreaks of violence at this nightclub, a 2016 Southtown Investigation revealed that Markham failed to mention Adrianna for any of the gun violence that had been happening there; instead, it was mentioned for using a fire hydrant without permission. The City went further to award the property developers more than $900,000 in tax breaks.

Additionally, former Mayor David Webb Jr was discovered to have spent $127,000 of campaign funds at Adrianna's banquet hall. He later stepped down from running for re-election following a federal investigation and confessed to taking bribes from city contractors after he was indicted on corruption charges in December 2017.

Adrianna also faced multiple lawsuits over the years, including the one brought by victim Ameer's aunt, Jennel Hooper. According to the lawsuit, which is still pending in the Cook County Court, Jennel alleged that the nightclub and its officials knew that it attracted a dangerous crowd but failed in their duty to provide adequate protection to ensure their customers' safety. In a similar lawsuit filed before Jennel Hooper, it was alleged that a man, Christopher Hooper, was *"trampled by a stampeding crowd of patrons"* after gunshots were fired. Both lawsuits were consolidated.

"Christopher Hooper's death is a tragedy that could have and should have been prevented," attorney James J. Gay, who was handling Hooper's lawsuit, said in a statement. *"This suit was filed to bring justice to Christopher's family, including his 5-year-old son who will now grow up without a father."*

Following the shooting that night, police described the chaos that night. An off-duty police officer had stopped at a nearby pizzeria on his way home when he noticed something was happening at Adrianna. He walked over there and found a man on the ground outside and in pain. He tried to create space for the man in pain because people were stepping over him to gain access into the club because the music continued to play non-stop despite the incident. The off-duty officer said, *"I had to raise my voice to tell (security guards) to shut that door,"* he said. *"And then, finally, I think, they shut it."*

Police and eyewitness accounts said shots were fired around 1 a.m. that Sunday at Adrianna's Sports pub on 163rd and Dixie Highway, killing 26-year-old Hooper and leaving another woman critically injured. A fight outside the club was said to have started before the gunfire.

According to William Stanback, an eyewitness at the venue, *"nothing happened at Billboard Live but there was shooting at the club next door- Addrianna's. They kicked us all out, about 40 minutes later they came in with shotguns and all kinds of stuff."*

The April 3 deposition named Ameer as the alleged shooter of Christopher Hopper, but no legal charges were filed against him until his death.

Hooper was known to authorities and had a criminal record for which he was on parole before he was murdered.

Chapter Twelve

Lil Durk – A Chicago Reigning Star

Lil Durk is a prolific Drill rapper who has made a pretty good name for himself despite his background. He has amassed more than 11 million Instagram followers and 5.5 million Twitter followers. He describes his songs as 'Melodized Drill.'

Durk Derrick Banks was born on October 19, 1992, in Chicago, Illinois. He grew up in the Southside Englewood neighborhood. His father's name is Dontay Banks Sr. His mother is only identified as a nurse. Durk's father was imprisoned when he was just seven years old, and as a result, he had massive responsibility at home. According to him, there were times when there was not enough food at home when he was younger.

After over two decades, Lil Durk reunited with his father, whom he fondly refers to as "Big Durk." He tweeted in February 2019, "Big durk home!!!!" adding a blue heart emoji. Photos showing his family having a meal together followed. His father was caught in a crack cocaine distribution and arrested in 1993. He was given two life sentences in July 1994, and after serving 22 years, he won his appeal. After nearly 25 years in prison, he was officially granted freedom. Before his release, Dontay Banks said:

"As it started out, I had a life sentence for the Stooge Pigeons who told on me. I been doing that time for 22 years now. But by the grace of Allah, I got that blessing and won the appeal and now I'll be out in a few years… to be with my boy, to be with my sons and be where I'm supposed to be in life and do the things I'm supposed to do as a Father."

Lil Durk said this about his dad:

"My daddy was one of the big guys. I seen a lot of it growing up… like I say my head was just everywhere. I'm like man 'I wanna be just like him'. They say he got caught with like eight million dollars and like six bricks."

In 2017, Durk moved to Atlanta, which has become the center of the hip-hop industry. He has six children – Angelo, Bella, Zayden, Du'mier, Willow, and Skyler.

Durk's Music Career

Durk discovered his interest in music while growing up, but he only took it more seriously in 2010, after becoming a father at 17 and dropping out of school. The rapper started his music career using Myspace and YouTube. His online fan base started to grow, and he grew fond of the idea of being a rapper.

Durk considered rapping as a full-time career after the release of his two singles – 'Sneak Dissin' and 'I'ma hitta' in 2011. In October 2012, he released his third mixtape, 'Life Ain't no Joke.' And in December of the same year, he released the track, 'L's Anthem,' which was remixed featuring French Montana.

'L's Anthem' got famous, and it led to a record deal with Def Jam Recordings, an American multinational record label with artists like Justin Bieber, Big Sean, and Kanye West, among others. In October 2013, Lil Durk released his fourth mixtape, 'Signed to the Streets.' Lil Durk summarized the mixtape in an interview:

"It's a lot more interesting. There's a lot more storytelling. It's different from my last mixtape but it's still real rapping. I just stepped it up a notch. I got DJ Drama and he made it bigger."

Rolling Stones, an American monthly magazine that focuses on music, politics, and popular culture, ranked 'Signed to the Streets' eighth on its list of the top 10 mixtapes in 2013. In June 2015, Lil Durk released his debut album, 'Remember My Name,' and the album peaked at number fourteen on the Billboard 200. He put out this sixth mixtape, '300 Days 300 Nights', in December of that year.

In 2018, Durk terminated his deal with Def Jam Recordings and started releasing his songs on Apple Music and iTunes. He signed to Alama Records and Interscope Records and released the album 'Signed to the Streets 3' in November 2018. His songs kept making it to the Billboard 200, with his 2020 mixtape, 'Just Cause Y'all Waited', ranking fifth. In April 2020, Durk made his first appearance on the Billboard Hot 100 with his single, 'Viral Moment.' In the same year, he featured in Drake's single, 'Laugh Now Cry Later,' which hit number two on the Billboard Hot 100.

After the death of his close friend, King Von, Lil Durk dropped 'Backdoor,' which was a tribute to his label mate. 'The Voice of the Heroes,' released with Lil Baby in May 2021, became his first release to debut atop the Billboard 200. Durk made an appearance on Kanye West's 'DONDA' and also contributed to Drake's 'Certified Lover Boy,' all released in 2021. According to Chart Data, Durk charted a total of 35 songs on the Billboard Hot 100 in 2021 alone. Lil Durk seems to keep breaking the boundaries every day. In an interview, he talks about his songs:

"Everybody reads about Chicago and the streets and I want to be that spokesperson. It's a good city with good artists. They've got to understand everything we went through to even get where we are now."

Gang Affiliation and Rap Sheet

Lil Durk is a member of the Black Disciples street gang. Soon after joining, he began getting into trouble with the law. In October 2011, he was sentenced to three months in jail for the possession of a firearm with a defaced serial number. He was later released on bond, only to be sent back to serve 87 more days.

In June 2013, Durk allegedly threw a loaded .40 mm caliber handgun into his vehicle. He locked it when police approached him on South Green Street in Chicago. Chicago police gained a warrant to search the car and found the loaded gun. He was arrested and held on a $100,000 bond. However, his lawyer claimed to have nine affidavits from witnesses who confirmed his innocence. Durk was released on July 18, 2013.

Durk was involved in a rivalry with Gangster Disciple member Joseph 'Lil Jojo' Coleman. In Durk's 'L's Anthem,' he insults Lil Jojo's gang set, the Brick Squad. Lil Jojo then responded with a diss track. The aftermath wasn't pleasant, leading to Lil Jojo's murder.

Lil Durk also had issues with Chief Keef's label, Glo Gang. After a social media exchange, Durk separated himself from Chief Keef's label, and as expected, hate songs followed. However, in August 2014, Durk decided to resolve his differences with Chief Keef.

Also, in 2014, Durk's dispute with California rappers, The Game and Tyga, began after they released their remix to Nicki Minaj's 'Chiraq.' Durk and The Game had heated exchanges on social media, and Durk responded with a Diss song, 'Bigger than Me.' Surprisingly, eight months later, Durk crushed his dispute with The Game and a week later with Tyga.

In September 2015, hours before a scheduled concert performance at the Theatre of Living Arts in Center City, Philadelphia, a shootout occurred, leaving Lil Durk's tour bus damaged and one man dead.

In June 2019, Lil Durk and King Von were accused of involvement in a February 2019 shooting outside an Atlanta restaurant. Durk was charged with attempted murder and aggravated assault, among other charges. After weeks in jail, Durk and Von were released on $250,000 and $200,000 bonds, respectively.

Durk and other rappers had made it a habit of name-dropping the dead in their songs. On Thursday, August 5, 2021, Lil Durk took to his Twitter account to declare his resolve to refrain from name-dropping the dead in his songs. He wrote in the tweet:

"I'm not mentioning the dead in my songs no more or performing songs with they name in it... big smurk".

Lil Durk suffered a string of losses due to gang and gun violence, and these losses hit him hard. On May 31, 2014, Lil Durk's cousin, 21-year-old McArthur 'OTF Nunu' Swindle, was fatally shot by mobsters in Chicago two days after signing to his record label. He was in one of Durk's SUVs when someone opened fire at him. The SUV crashed into a storefront afterward. Some believed Lil Durk was the target of that shooting.

On March 27, 2015, Durk's friend and manager, 24-year-old Uchenna 'OTF Chino Dolla' Agina, was shot dead. He was hit multiple times in the 8400 block of South Stony Island Avenue while sitting in a car. OTF Chino Dolla campaigned against mob violence in America and had a meeting with Joakim Noah to talk about anti-violence initiatives hours before his death.

Durk's relationship with King Von was deep and the loss hit him hard. Durk reportedly found out about Von's death during an Instagram Live session while previewing a new song that he had recorded. He made a post on Instagram, *"MY TWIN GONE. I LOVE YOU BABY BRO – D ROY!!!!"* along with a photo of King Von. After King Von's death and for unknown reasons, Durk deactivated his Instagram account. He came back to Instagram a while later.

As if Lil Durk had not seen enough death, Joshua Samuel, also known as 'Turn Me Up Josh,' died. His exact cause of death is not known. His death was revealed when Lil Durk shared a photo of him along with a caption that reads, *"Rip turn me up josh smh."* Turn me up Josh was a multi-platinum producer and engineer who received a Grammy nomination in 2020 for his work on Drake's and Durk's song, 'Laugh

Now Cry Later.' Lil Durk shared several pictures of himself working closely with Turn Me Up Josh on his Instagram story.

In the early hours of July 11, 2021, Durk and his girlfriend, India Royale, experienced a home invasion at their residence in the Chateau Elan neighborhood of Braselton, Georgia. Several unidentified individuals entered Durk's home in the early morning of July 11. Durk and his girlfriend reportedly exchanged gunfire with the unknown suspects. The Georgia Bureau of Investigation confirmed that neither Lil Durk nor his girlfriend was hurt during the shootout.

Not long after the news of Durk's home invasion broke out, 6ix9ine, a sworn rival of Lil Durk, commented, *"Y'ALL thought this man was gangsta. They sliding on this man every other week DAMN give him a break"* adding sideway crying laughing emojis. He added, *"SOMEONE SAID @lildurk not gon slide till they kill his girlfriend. YALL CRAZY"* with a crying laughing emoji.

After the home invasion, fans took to react to the news on Twitter. *"Durk and India the new Mr. & Mrs. Smith. That's goals,"* one tweeted. *"I'm weak. Lil Durk and India the new Bonnie and Clyde out,"* another shared.

Mr. & Mrs. Smith is a movie about a married couple where both of them were assassins. Bonnie and Clyde were an American couple known for their bank robberies and killings.

After the invasion, on July 20, Lil Durk posted on his Instagram story, *"Nobody should know everything you do cause they play role off what you do how you move and what you got."* Akademiks posted a screenshot of the story with the caption, *"#lildurk speaks. Is he speaking faxxxx or fiction?"*

Durk also posted, *"N****s don't even be with us that claim OTF so when ya'll do s**t to mfrs stand up for it don't leave us dry to deal wit it even tho we gone do us....half yall n****s bout to get the f**k on".* Virtually everyone who read the post found themselves confused, but Lil Durk and those concerned knew what he was trying to pass across.

Recent tweets from Lil Durk show his current thoughts. On September 7, he tweeted, *"I want another son !!!!"* and *"I be acting like I'm happy but I'm really sad inside"* with a sad emoji. His fans were in the comments section to console him and also give him words of advice.

Lil Durk lives on and continues to live in Atlanta, where he produces his music.

Characters like Lil Durk with massive social media followers can make a difference and start to end this dangerous lifestyle of gang rivals and shootings. Although he was born into this lifestyle, he now has a big voice, and he can do a lot more to curb the crime and the killings.

Dontay Banks Jr., popularly known as 'DThang,' is Lil Durk's older brother. Not much is known about him, but the fact that he was Lil Durk's brother brought him to the limelight. The two brothers were close and often seen together at events. His death brought deep sadness to his brother, especially after losing close buddies like King Von to gun violence.

DThang had two children with his girlfriend, identified as 'Fat Fat,' who had been with him for six years. He had a son, Dontay Banks III, and a daughter, Love.

DThang was killed on Sunday, June 6, 2021, when he was just 32 years old. The tragedy happened outside Club O, a strip club in the 17000 blocks of South Halsted, Harvey, Illinois, at approximately 12:20 pm.

Shortly before DThang was killed, a Harvey police officer heard gunfire and noticed a person with a gun in the club's parking lot. An altercation ensued with the unidentified suspect, and the officer was struck in the thigh by a stray bullet and was taken to the hospital.

Around the same time, police noticed shootings at the southeast corner of the club with return gunfire by unknown shooters at the northeast corner. The officers eventually found DThang near an SUV that was damaged by the gunfire. A large puddle of blood was found near his head and neck area, with multiple shell casings nearby.

According to Cook County officials, DThang was found dead on the 7900 block of S. Loomis Boulevard in Chicago. Some of his associates who were with him took him to South Suburban Hospital in Hazel Crest. The police officer was treated and discharged in good condition. Witnesses added that DThang got into an argument with an unknown man who shot him.

On the same night, police responded to a deadly shooting in the 100 block of West 155th Street, near Ingalls Memorial Hospital. The victim was 39-year-old Sinica Price, and the killing is believed to be in retaliation for DThang's death. She was taken to South Suburban Hospital in Hazel Crest, where she was pronounced dead.

From the analysis of DThang's shooting, there are some similarities with the killing of King Von; they were both shot in the parking lot of a nightclub. It sure happened to be coincidental.

On June 15, an arrest warrant was issued to 23-year-old Devinair English, who was allegedly involved in the police officer's shooting outside the Harvey strip club. According to court records and the Cook County state's attorney's office, the south suburban man was wanted for aggravated battery to a police officer and unlawful use of a weapon.

English was an associate of DThang who was fatally murdered in a separate shooting that happened around the same time in the club's parking lot. He was among those who accompanied DThang to the strip club that night and was allegedly involved in a physical altercation with the police officer, who noticed he had a handgun. No one is currently in custody for any of the shootings.

On the day of DThang's death, news broke that Lil Durk's older brother had been killed. Lil Durk remained silent on social media during the situation, which was a grieving moment for him. However, on Tuesday, June 22, he shared his first post on Instagram since his brother's death. Durk posted a picture of himself and his brother standing side by side with the caption *"DThang lil brother,"* adding an amplified speaker emoji. He turned off commenting on the post, likely to avoid any hurtful comments, especially from rival gangs and those who planned to mock his brother's death.

In response to DThang's death, a lot of tributes as well as consolations to Lil Durk and DThang's family were posted on social media. Chicago Media Takeout first shared a post relating to the killing. It read: *"Prayers to the person who got shot outside Club O. We have to start partying in peace."* Hours later, Urban News for Chicago confirmed the person who was killed in another post. *"Lil Durk's brother has been killed,"* was written above a photo of Durk and DThang. The caption read, *"Chicago, when is it going to stop? Durk, you're in our prayers. Most importantly praying for his kids."*

Calboy, a Chicago rapper, tweeted, *"R.I.P. DThang it's was always love when ya saw me."* He also responded to those making speculating comments about the incident:

"Bro ain't gone speak on nun but all these sacrifice jokes lame asf, u ain't never lived a real street life to know this s**t come with casualties on both sides. It's them pains that gets converted into motivations which lead to success. It's still pain. Let em grieve in peace".

Murda Beatz also tweeted, *"R.I.P. DThang."*

Chicago producer DJ L Beats took to social media to write:

"You advocated for me and my sound when most didn't and along with Leski positioned me to get my first and second album multi-placement credits with Durk. In this industry, you have few people who embrace young artist, producers, writers, etc. and give them equal shot with their

camp but you were one of those real men who did. I always appreciate your support and the power studio convos king".

Lil Reese posted: *"Long live dthang love you broski…"*

DThang's girlfriend and mother of his children shared an Instagram post expressing her grief. She posted a family portrait of herself, DThang, and their two children, along with a caption that reads, *"THIS WAS NEVER IN THE PLANS WTF! I LOVE YOU SOOOOOOOO MUCH".*

DThang's loved ones gathered for his funeral on Thursday, June 10. Pictures showed Durk gathered with his family for the event. All family members were dressed in white, and the burial took place according to the Muslim faith. The cover of the funeral program read, *"In our hearts forever."*

The Circle Continues

Like someone asked when DThang was killed, "When will the killing stop?" Unfortunately, it is difficult to answer that question because what we are dealing with is a culture. How do you cure a way of life? Will Chicago streets be cured of the cancer of crime, gangs, drugs, and gun violence that has become the nature of the people?

At 32, DThang was one of the few who lived to that age before being killed, whereas many died or were rotting in jail at half that age. There are even those who did not attain the phase of being teenagers when they were killed.

I guess the answer to "When will the killing stop?" may never be known.

Chapter Thirteen

More Deaths Around Lil Durk

McArthur Swindle - OTF NUNU

McArthur Swindle, known by his stage name, 'OTF Nunu,' is a rapper from Chicago. He is the cousin of Lil Durk, who signed him under his Only the Family (OTF). Nunu or Nuski, as his friends and family fondly called him, was born on December 15, 1992, in Chicago, Illinois. He lived in the 7200 Block of South Halsted Avenue in Englewood. His father was reportedly shot and killed in 1995.

Nunu was exposed to music by his parents and cousin. He gained popularity for his verses in Durk's 2014 single, 'OC,' released on April 14. The Source, an American hip-hop, and entertainment website describes the track and Nunu's performance:

"The track contains all of the attitude and toughness normally associated with the movement. While not much is known about NuNu, upon first listening, it becomes quickly evident that he can spit. His last verse is pretty serious and we look forward to hearing more of his music in the upcoming months."

OTF Nunu released a couple of songs before his demise. His tracks include 'Feeling Good,' 'At the Top,' 'DHK (Dillas, Hittas, Killas),' 'Used 2,' and 'Poundcake.' In addition to OC, Nunu has also been featured in 'Came from Nothing,' 'Rite Na,' 'Solo Dolo,' and 'Man Now.' He was preparing for his mixtape, 'Nuski Got Da Strap,' before his death. Merk Murphy, who owns the radio station where

Nunu was recording his new track, explained how successful it would have been.

"This was going to be his big breakout project. He was one of those kids who saw an opportunity to put himself in a better position with his music... Swindle's drill rap focused on his life. His songs were energetic, focused on having a good time and his relationship with people close to him," Murphy said.

On May 31, 2014, 21-year-old McArthur Swindle was shot in a parking lot in the 700 Block of East 87th Street, South Side Chicago. Around 3:20 pm, Nunu was seated in an SUV outside the Chatham Village Square Mall when an unidentified suspect approached him and fired multiple shots. He attempted to drive away from the scene but crashed into a storefront window. He was pronounced dead at the scene, at 3:25 pm, according to Cook Country Medical Examiner's Office.

The shooting appeared to be gang-related. It is also speculated to be retaliation for 20-year-old rapper Marc 'Lil Marc' Campbell, who was shot dead after releasing a video where he mocked OTF. No one has been arrested for Nunu's shooting. Hours before his murder, Nunu posted an image to his Instagram account with the caption, *"Im on some cool s**t."*

Words on the Street

Young Chop, a record producer famous for making Drill beats, tweeted that he had contacted Nunu just moments before the shooting. *"Just seeing him r.i.p lil bro,"* he posted on Twitter and Instagram.

Steve, a producer, and songwriter tweeted, *"@YoungChopbeatz and I were just talking to @OTF_NUNU then I get a call he was shot and killed. #wtf #chicago life is too short."*

Azea production also tweeted, *"Was Just Texting Bro smh RIP NuNu."*

Nunu's aunt, Sherri Swindle, told the Times that her nephew was not affiliated with any Chicago gangs. She also said that he was taking college courses in Joliet outside the City before his murder. She went further to plead for an end to gun violence, *"It needs to stop. He was a good person. He was a kindhearted person. He had a lot of soul."*

6ix9ine, known for dissing Chicago rappers, posted a video on Instagram of himself bringing flowers to Chicago's O Block, doing the sign of the cross, and kissing the ground. He wrote in the caption,

"CAME TO OBLOCK ... Came to pay my respect to @lildurk cousin nuski who was killed by gun violence. We need to change as a community #RIP NUSKI PRE ORDER THE ALBUM IN MY BIO SEPTEMBER 4TH."

Fellow OTF label signee, RondoNumbaNine paid respect to OTF Nunu from jail,

*"... OTF man, n****s know how we rocking. Got my page back, man. Rest in Peace, Nunu.."*

Durk was silent on social media following Nunu's death. A few hours before the shooting, he tweeted a link to 'OC,' a video featuring him and OTF Nunu. Days following Nunu's death, Durk issued a statement,

"Words can't explain @official_nuski just like you told me we gotta win......#Nuski." On June 3, 2014, Durk proceeded to honor his late cousin and thanked his fans for all their support.

"Nuski gang," *"I just turned my phone on and seen all dese text love for the support,"* he wrote in separate tweets. In an Instagram post, Durk wrote, *"This s**t really hittin me bro I wish you was here with me right now f**k everybody who ain't for us ily shorty on lss every tear I shed how many moms gone geel it."*

In his mixtape, '300 Days, 300 Nights,' released in December 2015, Durk remembers Nunu. He raps, *"I think I'm Nuski with the semi/He still got the strap, n****s trippin/And I'm hard body, man I miss him."*

In 2015, one year after Nunu's death, Durk posted a photo of Nunu on Instagram with a title, *"Regardless of The Pain I Ain't Gon Cry."* He captioned the post, *"Nuskiday rip my blood cousin man s**t crazy don't seem real wish you was here to see me killing s**t making n****s mad flexing on em I love ou lil bro I'm gone keep on f***ing em up #rememberMYNamealbumjune2nd p.s opps can't take me I'm doing tha most."*

On the 2nd anniversary of Nunu's murder, Durk shared a throwback photo of himself and his late cousin at two years old. He wrote in the caption, *"Me and nuski at 2yrs old all we use to wish was to be rich… r.i.p."* Durk also got a knuckle tattoo to memorialize his cousin.

Uchenna Agina - OTF CHINO

Uchenna Agina, known by his nickname 'Chino' or 'Chino Dolla,' was the manager of Lil Durk. His death was a blow to Durk and an addition to the numerous young people killed by gun violence in Chicago every year.

Chino was born in Nigeria and lived in the 7900 block of South Karlov Avenue in the Scottsdale neighborhood of Chicago. He was shot a few days after the release of Durk's track, 'Like Me,' featuring Jeremih, a single from his upcoming solo debut, 'Remember My Name.'

In the early hours of Friday, March 27, 2015, 24-year-old Chino went to a restaurant with his girlfriend to get food. While sitting in his red Chevy Camaro in Stony Sub restaurant at 8400 Stony Island Avenue, a man walked up to him with a gun and fired multiple shots at him. Police said he was hit several times, including once on the head.

According to Cook County Medical Examiner's office, he was taken to Advocate Trinity Hospital and later pronounced dead at 2:04 am. He wasn't the only victim of the shootout, but he was the only one killed because of the injuries he sustained. No one was arrested for the shooting.

A day before his death, Chino also posted a Lil Durk remix of 'Faneto,' a song originally produced by Chief Keef. The song mentions '300' and 'OBlock,' factions of the Black Disciple. It also attacks the 'Young Money' street gang.

In an interview, Lil Durk said he was on the phone with Chino about ten minutes before he was shot. He narrated,

"He told me 'finish up the album and the song called Why me.' He told me to just redo it for the label on my a**. I was like, 'I got you.' He was in the house laying down because I'll go Facetime with him. His girl called him ten minutes later."

He posted an Instagram picture with the caption,

"Rocking my drop chain for Chino and the rest we lost yall family in my prayers we staying strong still the king of Chicago album still drop may12th single on the radio streets can't stop me I'm still on my Lil Durk s**t #BON #OTF."

In a Twitter post, he added this voice to the anti-violence campaign,

"Put the guns down #Chicago," Lil Durk wrote.

He posted another photo on Twitter with a picture of Chino written 'Rest In Peace OTF Chino.' He captioned it, *"Rest Up big bro #OTFchino #milliondollern***a."*

DThang, Durk's brother tweeted,

"I Hard to Swallow. He Was A Business Man Wherever Business Was He Was Taking Care of it. My 20+ He Was My Brother && When I

Catch The Killer Ima Sit For Him Like the Lord Just Sent For Him #SleepTightChinoDolla #OnlyTheFamilyEnt @otf_Chino46 #MYNIGGA$LIFE."

Dreezy, tweeted, *"Thank you bro @OTF_CHINO,"* she wrote, adding three heart emojis.

Hustle Simmons wrote, *"RIP to my g @ otf_chino46... I literally spoke to him yesterday... F**k this violence got to stop.., this just f***ed my head up… praying for his family n my bro Durk."* He added in another post, *"RIP to my g… he was one of the good ones #rip chino."*

Dj Banz tweeted, *"Rip star playa 'Chino Diddy' @otf_chino46 #OTF."*

He further tweeted, *"S**t f***ed up but we gone remain focus and get to da top cuz diz wat was born to do #WeGoTeachother #OTF #RIPChino."*

Meek Mill posted, *"Damn bro!!"* with a picture saying Rest in Peace OTF Chino.

Chop Squad DJ posted, *"This cant be real. I swear, Bro as solid as they come. Rest easy Chino #chopsquad#otf."*

Youngchopbeatz also posted, *"Rip bro. I was on Facetime with last night s**t crazy #OTF @OTF_Chino46.*

A Def Jam Spokesperson wrote a statement paying tribute to Chino on Billboard,

"We are deeply saddened by the news of this tragedy. The Def Jam Family shares our most heartfelt sympathy, condolences and prayers with the family and loved ones of Uchenna Agina."

Devin Jackson, manager of Lil Durk's DJ, DJBanz, said, *"Chino was a good dude. He took care of business. That is what he was known for."* He also said he was the behind-the-scenes guy and referred to him as 'humble.' He went on to say that he met Chino on few days before his killing at a photoshoot for Lil Durk's upcoming album, 'Remember My Name.'

Chino's Campaign Against Gun Violence

Chino pushed the anti-violence initiatives for the 'Rock Your Drop' campaign organized by Chicago Bulls player Joakim Noah. According to an associate of the rapper, the shooting happened just hours after Chino met with Noah to talk about anti-violence initiatives. And a day before, he posted a group photo including Lil Durk and Noah. He captioned the post,

"It's always good when we link up with big bro @stickity13 @mattrmattr @theinterruptercobe @alexsperris #MajorMoves #Rock Your Drop."

Noah said he had never experienced anything like what happened with Chino and sent his condolences,

"I just know that somebody came to my house, and we were talking about doing some work for the kids and doing something positive. He got murdered. I never experienced anything like that. My respects go to his family and, to his friends. I just hope we can find solutions."

He also talked about why he must keep up with the anti-violence campaigns,

"What's going on in this city is very real. I signed up for this. I'm just like doing everything I can do to do something positive. Just need to keep up the good fight. I know everything I'm doing with my foundation comes from my heart. I think it's real important that we don't turn our backs on anybody... It's our movement, and we're very proud of it, and we just hope that it can spread. The more money we raise, the more programs we can put in for these kids. It's a harsh reality here in Chicago. Violence is out of control."

Noah formed 'Rock Your Drop' to address the high level of gun violence in Chicago. The drop pendants used in the movement help to spread the message of positivity and non-violence. Lil Durk also joined the campaign and posted a video on Twitter supporting 'Rock Your Drop.' He captioned it, *'Save your city support the movement #RockYourDrop #Cureviolence @noahsarcfdn @theinterruptercobe."* In the video, he said, *"It's your boy Lil Durk live from Chicago. When you 'Rock Your Drop,' just know your neighborhood is safe. Stop the violence movement. Salute my fans, salute my followers."*

Devonshe Collier – THF ZOO

Devonshe Collier, also known as 'THF Zoo,' 'Bayzoo,' or 'Baybay,' is a Chicago rapper based in Atlanta. He is signed under the Only the Family (OTF) label and had a close relationship with Lil Durk and King Von. THF Zoo is known as one of the top "hittas" in his gang, THF 46. Devonshe was born on September 26, 1991, on the North Side of Chicago. He lived in one of the most dangerous apartment complexes in Chicago before moving to the Woodlawn neighborhood. He is the elder brother of Lil Gudda and is said to have three kids.

THF Zoo is a notorious member of the Black Disciple set, THF (Trigger Happy Family) 46. which includes Black Disciple and Mickey Cobra gang members. The name was adopted after the death of one of its members, 'Trigga.' Zoo was said to have joined the gang when he was 12. He had been associated with gang activities from a young age.

Music Career

THF Zoo started to take music more seriously in 2020, after his release from jail. On May 7, he released his song 'The Streets Bleed Murder.' Afterward, he dropped many more including, 'Safe,' 'All Type of S**t,' and Christmas (featuring Dee Mula).

Zoo has been featured in 'Do it for Von,' 'Get Backers,' 'Sip Again,' and 'White Rocks Green

Weed.' His albums include 'The Streets Bleed Murder' and 'Murder.' He also did a song, 'Back in Blood Remix,' with his daughter.

At 18, THF Zoo was a suspect in the shooting to death of 21-year-old Dominic Barnes on July 5, 2009. The murder took place in the Bronzeville neighborhood. THF Zoo was arrested on November 7, 2014, over five years later, at Southwest Suburban Orland Park, home of rapper Lil Durk. Lil Durk was arrested for weapons violation after police found two loaded guns in his house. Zoo had a pending unlawful use of a weapon case from January 2014 at the time of his arrest.

Prosecutors said the late victim was standing outside when Devonshe approached him and asked about his gang affiliation. After Dominic's reply, he brought out a gun and fired multiple shots at him. Afterward, THF Zoo and an unidentified co-defendant went through Dominic's pocket and removed money before fleeing into a waiting vehicle.

Multiple witnesses identified THF Zoo as the shooter. And at least one witness reported seeing him with the gun immediately after the shooting. He served about four years for the charges and was set free in January 2018 for lack of evidence on the case.

Zoo was arrested on a warrant a few months after he left jail. This was when he and King Von recorded the song, 'Beat that Body,' amassing almost 7 million views as of 2021. On April 5, 2019, Zoo was arrested again for reckless conduct and having a rifle and a shotgun. He was released on bond a few days later.

On May 13, 2019, Zoo was arrested again for the murder of Dominic Barnes. It was around the same time that King Von and Lil Durk were both arrested for an attempted murder charge. However, a little more than a year later, on March 22, 2020, THF Zoo was released.

THF Zoo was sometimes cordial with Yarmel '051 Melly' Williams, a member of the 051 Young Money gang and one of the top gang's top "hittas." 051 Young Money is one of THF 46 biggest rivals. Zoo did a lot of live video sessions with 051 Melly. Zoo says he likes 051 Melly because he has the ball to himself. In a live video with Zoo, Melly told him that if killing weren't illegal, he'd spit on him when he was done.

051 Melly was shot to death in September 2019 while attending a party in Jaro City. Many believe friendly gang members set him up. Police soon named Nate, a Tyquan World (TW) gang member, as a suspect in his death.

THF Zoo took to Instagram live to mourn 051 Melly. He said, *"miss my boy melly he was real one Krump was a goffy."* Krump, known as MUBU Krump, was a close friend of 051 Melly and a member of the Gangster Disciples. Krump was also known for his feuds with rival gang members. He and Melly were shot outside a house party in Chicago, but only Melly survived the shooting.

Zoo was also friends with THF Raheem, a fellow gang member. In May 2015, Raheem was shot while leaving a restaurant. He ran into an alley where he collapsed and died. Witnesses identified Arieus Fitch as Raheem's killer. Raheem was murdered when he was just 15.

THF Zoo speaks on a 4-year-old getting killed through his Instagram account,

*"You new n****s don't understand the concept of war from my knowledge it's gone be tragedy on both sides ain't no such thing as a win but when it*

comes to killing these innocent women and kids I ain't never ben with none of that's**t ain't no respect behind that s**t ion care wat u think u is and y'all homies lame asl if y'all comin back from slidin and They ain't put u in the blender once they got the news because that's exactly We a you'll be f***in with me."

The four-year-old was shot in the head. According to police, bullets fired outside his father's Woodlawn house flew in through the open window, hitting him.

Devonshe has been posting photos and videos of King Von, asking his fans to follow Von's page for more posts. He also used the hashtags, '#longlivekingvon,' '#longlivevroy,' and '#onlythefmaily.'

Chapter Fourteen

Big Glow Got Deemed

Mario Hess - BIG GLO

Mario Hess, known by his stage name, Big Glo, is the cousin of Chief Keef. He was formerly known as Blood Money. Hess was born on February 13, 1984, in Chicago, Illinois.

Hess grew up in Southside Englewood, and according to him, growing up in that area was scary. He frequently got into trouble with some 'big bosses' on the streets. In an interview, Hess recounted an experience he had when he was younger, *"I was rebellious, ain't want to listen. I thought I could do my own thing. They caught up with me one day, and on my way to crib, they chased me down. I had to stop. They stump me out and put me in the hospital. I was in a hospital for a couple of months… I was messed up. My mouth was wired shut."*

Big Glo talked about his street life experience, *"I didn't come up with a mother and father like everybody else. I came up with the streets, guns and money and drugs. I always felt like I was the s**t cos I was like the youngest guy on the block serving s**t. I always had money. When the big guys got paid, I got paid too, so they kind speak for my attitude. I'm kind of cocky."*

When asked about his view of younger kids involved in gun violence, he says, *"It's a free ball game. The best man win in Chicago. They play for keeps, so it's like the older guys, they smart. They're looking at it like 'Okay if I can get these shorties to go ahead and do it, I can save myself a jail sentence, I can glow them up and make them feel like they straight, make them feel like they high, give them guns and the globe and they're going to start shooting.' It's different than when I came up. When I was 18, 17, 16, I was doing time for something I did at 12 and 11, so I hadn't have time to experience what they experienced growing up.'"*

Big Glo became active in music in 2013 and was signed under Glory Boyz Entertainment (GBE), now known as Glo Gang. He was the eldest member of the GBE. Glo released several mixtapes centered around street life that won him a following in the drill scene and attracted the attention of Interscope Records.

Big Glo's mixtape, 'Drug Wars,' was released for GBE in 2013 before signing to Interscope Records, the same label that signed his cousin two years before. He released numerous tracks which include, 'Thought He Was,' 'Nino Brown,' 'What I Do,' and 'Savage.' Big Glo also appeared in Chief Keef's 'F**k Rehab' in 2013.

According to Glo, he always had a way with words and had been rapping since he was 11. Tupac was one of those that played a part in his music career. Glo's manager, Renaldo Hess, said he changed his rap name to 'Big Glo' because 'Blood Money' was trademarked.

In an interview, Hess was asked why people easily gravitated toward Chief Keef. He replied, *"He's speaking reality. He's speaking the reality of so many Society. He's speaking what everybody want to do. What everybody trying to do. What everybody going through. He's a product of his environment but he like the great white hope. You see him you know you can make it like this… I learn a lot from him. He's a real smart dude."*

He also added that Keef used to tell him how he wanted to work for him when Keef was younger, but he always told Keef to go to school because he didn't want to see him do all he did.

Chief Keef revealed that Big Glo was a member of the Gangster Disciples. He wrote,

"@bigggglo A true Gang Member And He Was GDN!!!! His lil cousin a 2-4 member!!! My cousin will live through me I ain't gotta say s**t listen to my new s**t u a see."

Big Glo had a lengthy arrest record, including drug cases and weapon offenses. Records show he had been arrested dozens of times and served time for multiple crimes over 12 years.

Hess talked about how he grew into a life of crime,

"Before I went to jail, my family had a lot of money. I came up around a lot of big-time drug dealers with money, so I ain't really had to do a lot. At 11, I caught a case for possession of control substance. I got caught with like ninety bags of crack cocaine, and I went to the penitentiary… I was fighting that case until like 14, then I went to jail. The judge sentenced me to originally four months, but I ain't come home for like 46 months. I caught more in-house cases."

In September 2002, 18-year-old Hess was charged with manufacturing and delivering cocaine. He pled guilty, and some of the charges were dropped. He was sentenced to a year in jail. In 2007, Hess pled guilty to a case of weapon violation, including aggravated battery and possession of a firearm by a felon. He was given a two-year jail sentence. In a more recent case, Hess was sentenced to two years probation and was accused of violating the probation about eight months later.

On Wednesday, April 4, 2014, Hess visited the 5600 block of South Elizabeth Street where his family's home was located. He had gone to celebrate the birthday of two of his cousins, not knowing it would be his last day. Hess and his cousin, Darnell Patton, were standing in front of Hess' truck and talking to some girls when unknown gunmen came up and started shooting. The shooting left Hess with multiple gun wounds.

Police said two shooters opened fire just south of 56th Street on Elizabeth Avenue around 9:45 p.m. on Wednesday, leaving more than two dozen shell casings in the street. Hess was reportedly shot at least ten times.

Upon arrival at John H. Stroger Jr. Hospital, Hess was pronounced dead. His cousin, who was shot in the abdomen, underwent surgery overnight, and his condition had stabilized by the next day. Nobody was charged with the shooting.

On Friday, April 18, 2014, Hess' burial ceremony took place in the Holy Temple Cathedral in Harvey. He was buried in Mount Hope Cemetery. A memorial was also set up at the scene of the shooting. A day after Glo's death, more than a dozen of his friends and family gathered on porches, sidewalks, and inside cars on the block where the shooting occurred. Some held posters scribbled with tributes.

"I miss you dearly," one read.

"Half of my heart gone," another stated.

Big Glo's manager and cousin, Renaldo Reuben Hess, said,

"He was excited and just glad to tell people, 'man I'm signed with Interscope now. I told you I was going to do it,' and all that stuff... I had a feeling something like this was going to happen. That was the whole reason for us trying to get him to move... I told him, 'You need to stay off the streets. We need to try to get Interscope to get you the rest of your money so you can move.'"

He added that Hess wasn't shy about flashing his newfound wealth, which included thousands of dollars in cash, big diamond bracelet rings, a gold chain, and a Denali truck. Hess' manager added, *"I just spoke to him two days ago, and I could sense something wasn't right. Whenever you get money, people in Chicago start looking. They didn't have money, and he was flashing $8,000. Other people looking to stick him up."*

His manager said he wanted to move – possibly to Los Angeles, where he'd recorded songs for Interscope, but he didn't have enough money. He wanted to move his entire family including his children.

Renaldo also added that Glo didn't take his music career seriously, *"He wanted to do it, but the streets were paying him. He was in and out of jail, selling drugs, stuff like that. It's a lot of crime and violence in Chicago. Those rap gangs are being targeted, so you know, just trying to get him outside the neighborhood. He's from the streets. He was basically trying to get his rap career together because that's a good opportunity. They gave him some money upfront. It was a good chance for him to get himself out of the hood... He was trying to get the rest of the money and stay off the streets, you know."* Hess' manager also gave some good remarks about him, *"A lot of people that don't know him and just listened to his music don't know what type of person he was. He was a very funny person. He was a very loving person."*

Condolences started pouring in on Twitter after the shooting of Big Glo.

Big Glo's neighbor, Tarsha Glenn, commented on his humility,

"He wasn't one of those types where he felt he made it, and he was too good for us. He was right here with us still, day before yesterday. That's how he got killed last night because he's representing his hood."

Allena Taylor, a relative of Glo, explained that Hess was killed out of jealousy,

"He made it. He made it, and they was mad... He had a lot of people of him, and it's sad. He came from nothing to that, look at him. He didn't deserve that at all; neither one of them, Darnell neither."

Allena also added that he deserved and worked hard for his getting signed into Interscope Records.

"Like you see stuff on Instagram and stuff, jealous of him because he made it. He deserved that. He worked hard. Those were rhymes out of his mouth."

Fredo Santana tweeted, *"Rip Blood Money ima miss you cuzo."*

Rapper Edai wrote, *"RIP BLOODMONEY."*

Matti posted a photo of himself, Tray Savage, and Big Glo, with the caption,

"Dey Jus Took My Big Cuzin I Love U Cuzo Im Gone Miss U I Swea We Had So Much Planned We Was Finna Take Ova Mannn Idk Wht To Say u Was BigGlo BloodMoney Da Boss U Made Me Feel Safe Around Whteva I Love U Always Imma Do Tht Verse 4 U Saturday Cus I Know How U Was Finna Come Cuz Mannnn I Was Jus WishinThis Did Not Happn We Jus Tlk To U 30 mins b4 Dey Called Us I Always LovU Big Cuz Glod All Up Put Da Cameras On Me!"

Lil Herb captioned a photo of Big Glo,

*"ON VITO BIGGLO YOU WAS MY MANZ REST UP GANG ON FOENEM N****S HATE MORE THAN THEY BREATHE NOWADAYS,"*

DJ Faze tweeted, *"RIP Glo Gang Affiliate Rapper Blood Money, He Was Shot Multiple Times and Passed Away At A Nearby Hospital."*

Big Glo's father, Richard Holmes, expressed his guilt for the tragic death of his son,

"I was a gang leader. This is a product of what we created. As the elders we created this. So now we got to undo some of this. My son is laying in there now from the violence we set... You can say I blame myself. When my kids were coming up, they seen their daddy. Whenever they seen me, they know that I was a strong man back then, but I was in a gang. I was in the Stones. He ended up being a disciple."

Holmes pointed to the scar on the back of his shaved head, a reminder of his failed attempt to get out of gang life years ago.

"It's all going to be positive. It ain't gonna be about no rap, not gonna be about no record labels, no deals or none of that. It's gonna be about my son's legacy… and making it mean something, other than just another black man gone."

XXL Mag, an American hip-hop magazine, wrote,

"What makes Big Glo's demise even sadder is that his life was beginning to take a positive turn. As someone who spent a lot of time in the streets, Glo's music was leading him away from his past. Just weeks before his death, his collab with Chief Keef 'F**k Rehab'; amongst his other music caught the attention of Interscope Records, who signed him in. Rest in Peace, Big Glo."

Chief Keef described how his cousin's death affected him in an interview with Billboard,

"When that happened that was the biggest lesson. It told me, 'You gotta grow up.' I know he would want me to be a better person. To do better. When [his murder] happened, it's like [his spirit] jumped in me. How he rocked, he used to just go crazy, saying all types of stuff. He brought me back."

Keef also created a new Big Glo chain to memorialize his late cousin. He also promised fans new music from Glo shortly following his death. He posted, *"Finna Drop My Cousin Blood Money Song – Believe Ina Glo."* As promised, on April 13, 2014, the song was released.

Chapter Fifteen

Lil Reese and Fredo Santana – One Dead, the Other Has Nine Lives

Tavares Lamont Taylor, known by his stage name, Lil Reese, is a rapper from Chicago. He is one of the pioneers of Chicago's Drill music and a Black Disciples gang member. He was born on January 6, 1993, and raised in Chicago's South Side. He dropped out of high school to pursue his music career. Reese is known for his collaborations with popular drill artists Chief Keef, Lil Durk, and Fredo Santana. He was a part of Glory Boyz Entertainment (GBE).

He gained recognition after featuring in Chief Keef's 2012 single 'I Don't Like' which peaked at 73 on Billboard Hot 100 and 20 on Hot R&B. He gained widespread attention and in the same year, released his debut mixtape, 'Don't Like.' Reese caught the attention of American record producer, No I.D. who led him to sign with the hip-hop record label, Def Jam Recordings in 2012. After the signing, Def Jam President, Joie Manda said in a statement,

"Lil Reese brings a gritty, authentic perspective to life on the streets of Chicago. Artists like Reese are part of our lifeblood here at Def Jam, where we not only cherish our heritage as the definitive label in Hip Hop, but seek out, sign and develop the freshest talent our culture has to offer."

In 2012, he released a remix for his song, 'Us,' featuring Rick Ross and Drake. The track later appeared in Ross' mixtape, 'The Black Bar Mitzvah.' He released his second mixtape, 'Supa Savage' in 2013, featuring guest appearances from Chief Keef, Lil Durk, Fredo Santana, and Wale. Since then, he has released five mixtapes, 'Supa

Savage 2,' '300 Degreez,' 'Better Days,' 'GetBackGang,' and 'GetBackGang2.' His popular singles include 'Us' and 'Traffic.'

Not much is known about Reese's family, but on June 15, 2014, he welcomed his first daughter, Aubri Taylor. In June 2020, he shared a photo of his daughter during her 6th birthday. He captioned the photo,

"Happy bday to my baby she gettin big on me"

Lil Reese has been involved in several legal issues. In May 2010, he pleaded guilty to burglary charges and was given two years of probation. In April 2010, he was charged with driving without insurance and a driver's license and he was issued a traffic violation for not signaling.

On October 24, 2012, a video that allegedly showed Lil Reese brutally beating a woman was brought to the spotlight. The video was posted on various Hip Hop websites. According to the Chicago SunTimes, *"In the video, a young woman asks who let the group of young men into a home. She begins to argue with a young man and seconds later the young man, purported to be Def Jam Recordings rapper Lil Reese, gets close to the young woman and viciously starts punching her. A few seconds into the beating, she begins to shriek, 'Wait,' her voice breaking as she begins to cry."*

The video triggered opposing gang members to start disrespecting Reese in videos. Police did not initially investigate the case relating to the video because they did not know who the victim was, when the incident occurred or where. Reese made a Twitter post commenting on the video, *"The haters tryna see a mf Dwn lol Dey gotta b broke and bored wanna upload sum s**t from years ago damnn we winnin it's 2 late...#3hunna."*

On April 28, 2013, Reese was arrested by Chicago police on a warrant while sleeping in a car. The warrant was connected to charges of criminal trespass to a residence with persons present, mob action, and battery that allegedly took place in February 2012. He was held on a $100,000 bond.

On June 23, 2013, he was arrested in Chicago and charged with motor vehicle theft. According to court records, he failed to provide ownership documentation of the luxury vehicle when he was stopped in April 2013. The charge was later dropped.

On July 23, 2013, 20-year-old Lil Reese was arrested again for possession of marijuana which violated his probation. He was arrested on a sidewalk in Englewood with a reported four grams of the substance. The police report also added that he had over $2000 cash with him. It quoted Reese's explanation for the materials in his possession, *"It's mine, I got a little weed. So what?... There's serious crime out there. This ain't a big deal. I'm gangster."*

In August 2014, Reese was locked up for felony possession of a firearm. In January 2016, he was arrested on indirect criminal contempt charges an arrest that originated from the 2014 arrest.

On November 11, 2019, Lil Reese was shot in the neck and listed in critical condition. Witnesses said he was pursued by the driver of another car during a chase, and as many as 12 gunshots were fired. The driver got out of the car, shot Reese, and fled the scene. The shooting happened at a busy intersection in the area of Markham and Country Club Hills. An unknown man took Reese to a hospital nearby Hazel Crest, where he was treated, stabilized, and transferred to Advocate Christ Medical Centre in Oak Lawn.

After the shooting, police came to the scene and found a car with fresh blood in the driver's seat and on the ground close to the car. Nobody was arrested for the shooting.

On November 17, he shared the good news of his well-being on Instagram by sharing a photo showing his stitched neck. He captioned it, *"Made 4 it Lifes a gamble I got hella luck."*

He also wrote a tweet to thank everyone who supported him during his hospitalization,

"I appreciate everybody keeping me in they prayers tho I can't lie thank y'all no matter what you do out here always talk to god."

A week after surviving the fatal shooting, he released 'Come Outside,' a song he recorded before he was shot. According to Billboard, *"the new song chronicles the danger all around."* Reese had also been updating his fans on when he would return to the studio, stating that he was unable to speak for the time being.

On May 15, 2021, Reese was shot again, but this time, he wasn't seriously wounded. He was allegedly involved in a carjacking that ended in a shootout. The shooting which occurred in a parking garage in the River North neighborhood involved a group of men. When the police arrived, they found the three men with gunshot wounds and the stolen Dodge Durango littered with bullets. The three men were taken to the hospital with only one in serious condition. Reese suffered a graze to his eye, head, and mouth. The other two men were shot in their knee and torso respectively.

Details from police suggest that Reese was wounded in a gunfight that occurred after a 55-year-old man tracked his son's stolen car to a garage in the first block of West Grand Avenue and tried to take the car from them. The son had directed his father by using a GPS tracker in the car, and his cellphone, police said.

As the father confronted Reese and others inside the car, another person appeared and opened fire on the car. The police said the car sped off and crashed, and the occupants of the car exchanged gunfire with the other shooter. Three men were wounded in the shootout, including Lil Reese. Numerous shell casings were found at the scene, and multiple weapons were found inside the stolen Dodge Durango. Lil Reese reportedly told authorities that he was only there to purchase marijuana.

A graphic video showing a part of the aftermath of the shooting circulated on social media. The voice of the woman recording the video and a man is heard yelling at another man who was bloodstained and was walking out of a parking garage. Another man, identified as Lil Reese because of his tattoos, was seen lying against a wall behind a barrier. He appeared to be breathing heavily as a police officer tried to talk to him and called for an ambulance.

At about 5 p.m. on that day, a post was made to Reese's Instagram story, *"Everyone Keep praying for reese & his family."*

On May 20, the 28-year-old rapper took to Snapchat to talk about the rumors flying around concerning the shooting,

"I'm good. I'm not blind or shit. Don't believe what you seeing on [the] internet. I don't even kno where tf they getting all these fake ass stories from."

The next day, he wrote another message on Twitter, *"Errtime I feel like my back against the wall I*

come out in better position so I ain't tripping."

In a three-part interview with Fucious TV, Reese said that the shooting went down *"outside of the Grand Plaza apartment."* He continued, *"I got grazed in the eye, I got grazed in the head, and I got grazed in the mouth… It was never no fighting going on. Like, the dude that was recording me was just lying saying, 'Oh it's a fight.' No, it wasn't no fighting going on, they was saying that probably to cover their a** cause the police was right there, and they called the police as I got downstairs from getting shot. The people I was getting weed from pulled into the garage. I was trying to get out."*

He explains his side of the story of what happened in the scene,

"So as they're shooting up the car, now they're running away. I'm tryna run out the car, now, as I'm coming out the garage, it's people running up with their phones. It's a b***h running up with her phone and a n***a

running up with their phones telling the police, 'Yeah he stole our car, he stole our car.' Now, the police come slam me on the ground and make me hit my head on the pole that was right there. Now, I'm dazed and shit cause where I was bleeding and all that [was because] the police knocked me down 'cause they were running up saying I stole their car."

He also said he wasn't arrested because he didn't commit the crime. *"I never got arrested, I just went to the hospital... I ain't get arrested for none of that s**t 'cause I ain't steal no car or no s**t like that."*

In March 2020, Reese posted a tweet that blamed the Chinese people for the Coronavirus outbreak. He posted,

"Chinese people nasty asl man got the whole Earth globe f**k up,"

The comment section was filled with people either making fun of the post or describing the post as 'racist' or inappropriate. As a result of the tweet, his twitter account was suspended. He took to Instagram to post a screenshot of the official violation notification from Twitter with a caption,

"Lol Look how the Chinese people did my Twitter."

On May 29, 2021, Reese was arrested at home after his girlfriend reported him to the police for alleged domestic violence. According to the police report, Reese was accused of pulling his girlfriend's hair and striking her in the face with his closed fist. She suffered bruises on her lips which were visible to police officers. He was charged with misdemeanor domestic battery but later released on a $10,000 bond a few hours later. He denied laying hands on his girlfriend. In an interview, he described the incident as fake and that it was just an argument, *"That s**t was fake. That was just an argument going on. Somebody seen us arguing and called the police, so when the police came they already knew who I was. So they were like, 'Aight, we finna just lock him up.'"*

Lil Reese is fortunate to be one of those who have escaped death but will he stay away from the crime and violent life that has sent thousands of young Chicago boys to jail or to early graves? I guess only time will tell.

Derrick Coleman – Fredo Santana

Fredo Santana, born Derrick Coleman, is the older cousin of Chief Keef. He is known as one of the pioneers of Chicago's Drill music and is well known for his music style and the tattoo of a cross on his forehead. He is associated with the Black Disciples street gang and used the names '300' and '3hunna' in many of his songs.

Santana began his music career in 2011 when he was 21. He was signed under Glory Boyz Entertainment (GBE) and is best known for his appearance in Drake's 2013 music video, 'Hold on We're Going Home,' where he played a man who kidnaps Drake's on-screen girlfriend.

After the release of his first mixtape, 'It's a Scary Sight' in September 2012, he started becoming known in Chicago's Drill scene. The mixtape featured guest appearances from Lil Reese, King L, Lil Durk, Gino Marley, Frenchie, and his cousin, Chief Keef. His second mixtape, 'Fredo Krueger,' was released in February 2013.

In October 2013, he released his debut album, 'Trappin Ain't Dead' which peaked at number 45 on the US Billboard 200. The album also debuted Santana's label imprint, Savage Squad Records. He released music regularly until his final release, 'Fredo Krueger 2,' his second studio album, in September 2017. He scheduled a release of a collaborative mixtape with Chief Keef, 'Turbo Bandanna,' but it was postponed because he was hospitalized.

Billboard explained how Fredo Santana began to gain recognition, *"Santana's name was cemented into the minds of rap fans through his younger cousin Chief Keef's 2012 breakout hit "I Don't Like," in which Keef made an inimitable mention of Santana in his verse: "Fredo in the cut/ That's a scary sight." The song, later remixed by Kanye West, catapulted Keef and Santana's Glory Boyz Entertainment squad, drill music, and new trends in Chicago rap more broadly into the national spotlight."*

Santana was a heavy drug user. He was said to be addicted to Xanax and Lean. He attributed his addiction to a trauma he experienced during his childhood. He revealed that he had Post Traumatic Stress Disorder (PTSD) and turned to drugs as a coping mechanism.

In October 2017, after his second hospitalization, he spoke about why he got used to hard drugs through his Twitter handle and considered going to rehab,

"I was running from my old life tryna get high didn't want to face them demons."

*"Hopefully I can be the face to sho n****s to slow down an we got our whole life ahead of us f**k being rock stars gettin high I got ptsd... I'm getting help I might just go to rehab."*

He was rushed to the hospital in March 2017 after suffering a seizure. He posted a picture of himself on a hospital bed with patches and wires attached to his chest on Instagram. He wrote a caption, *"When u working hard no sleep u get sleep deprived an have a light seizure."* Fans assumed his love for Lean could have been the cause of his hospitalization.

In September 2017, Russ, another Drill rapper, posted a picture of himself wearing a T-shirt that read, 'How much Xans and Lean do you have to do before you realize you're a fucking loser' on Twitter.

In another tweet, Russ commented on why he did what he did,

"If I stopped ONE kid from abusing xans or lean, mission accomplished.. better than getting ONE kid to try that shit. Period."

A lot of Twitter users talked about the message on the T-shirt. But Santana's reply explained why he couldn't stop abusing the drugs.

"Until I can stop thinking bout my dead homies an the trauma that I been thru in my life that's when I'll stop."

Santana's seizures continued, and he was diagnosed with idiopathic epilepsy in May 2017. He still suffered multiple seizures despite the prescription drug he was given to combat them. In October 2017, a friend and fellow rapper, Gino Marley, found Santana mid-seizure on the floor of his house with blood coming from his mouth. He was rushed to the hospital and diagnosed with liver and kidney failure.

He posted on his social media handle,

"Been in here since Friday doctor say a n***a had kidney failure an liver failure. Gino found me on da floor shaking bleeding out the mouth having a seizure s**t could a been the end."

He also wrote about why he wasn't going to be releasing any of the album he was scheduled to release,

"I'm getting back to normal sorry to all my fans turbo bandana will not be dropping tomorrow due to my health issue. Thanks for everyone who prayed for a nigga I wouldn't wish this on my worse enemy."

Two days later, Santana said that he was *"out of the hospital"* and *"on my way to the studio."*

Sadly, on January 19, 2018, three months after he was diagnosed with kidney and liver failure, he was discovered unresponsive in his home in Reseda, Los Angeles by his girlfriend. He had suffered a seizure that took his life around 11 pm that night.

Autopsy reports show that the major cause of the rapper's death was cardiovascular disease and idiopathic epilepsy was listed as a contributing factor.

Record producer and rapper, Maxo Kream, was the first to break the news of Santana's death on Instagram. He posted Santana's picture with a caption,

"Damn man I'm lost for words right now I'm cryin my ass off Fredo I love yu B***h RIP a real Savage."

Drake posted, *"Rest in Peace Santana."*

Lil Durk also paid tribute to the rapper,

"This one f***ed my head up I can't even lie rest up young king @FREDOSANTANA300."

Chief Keef took to Twitter to dismiss rumors saying that his cousin died from drug addiction,

"N****s say my cousin died of lean again and he didn't I'm f**king beating the ass."

Keef also made a post emphasizing that Santana was his cousin,

"Stop saying Fredo was my friend, That's my cousin, Big difference."

Andrew Barber, who runs the hip-hop site FakeShoreDrive, said in an emailed statement,

"I met Fredo in early 2012, just as Chicago's Drill boom was taking off. Despite how he may have been perceived by media or the fans, Fredo was one of the kindest and coolest artists I've come in contact with during my 10+ years in the business. He had a clear plan of what he wanted to do and how he wanted to accomplish it. … His flow, look and style was often mimicked and imitated throughout the years, but the industry recognized him as an originator and innovator. He will be missed."

Barber also tweeted,

"R.I.P. @FREDOSANTANA300. Legitimately one of the nicest and coolest dudes I crossed paths with while working in this crazy biz. Prayers to him and his family. Terrible news."

Glory Boyz Entertainment issued a statement to Billboard,

"Everyone at Glory Boyz Entertainment is shocked and saddened by the sudden passing of Fredo. He was not only a talented rapper but family to everyone and a true star who was taken too soon. We are all proud of everything he was able to accomplish in his life and he will truly be missed. At this time we ask for privacy and prayers for his family and friends."

A few months after his death, a music video for 'Demons,' a track from Santana's 2017 album, 'Fredo Krueger 2,' was released. And on September 2019, his partner, Audrey Scott, uploaded a clip for *'Some Money,'* a track from the 2017 mixtape 'Pluggin In.'

Chapter Sixteen

Carlton Weekly, aka FBG Duck

Carlton Weekly, aka FBG Duck, was born on September 6, 1994, in the Woodlawn neighborhood of Chicago. He is a Drill rapper whose songs focused mainly on the Drill scene and a member of the rap group Fly Boy Gang also known as Clout Boyz. Members are mainly from the Gangster Disciples and other gang members include Lil Jay, Young Mello, Cashout, Dutchie, and Billionaire Black. The crew has released several songs insulting the rival rappers such as Chief Keef and C-Dai.

Duck began his music career at the age of 17 but rose to prominence in 2018 with his single, 'Slide.' His hit single was remixed by 21 Savage and led to a recording contract. He has since released numerous solo singles and projects with his Fly Boy Gang rap crew within the last five years.

Following the success of his 2018 single, Duck signed a record deal with Sony Music Entertainment and afterward released an extended play, 'Big Clout.' He declared his excitement in a 2018 interview with VladTV, *"I ain't gonna lie to you, I'm actually happy as hell. I'm proud of myself."*

In 2016, Duck released his first mixtape, 'Look At Me.' He dropped the second, 'Different Personalities' in 2015, followed by its sequel, 'Different Personalities 2' in 2017. The mixtapes featured appearances from Billionaire Black, Rooga, and others. He released a two-project-long series called 'How I'm Coming' in 2016 and 2017. His final two releases, 'Look at Me 2' and 'Big Clout,' came out in 2018, featuring guest appearances from FBG crew such as FBG Dutchie and FBG Young.

Duck revealed during his The Break interview with XXL that he wasn't the kind of person people think he is. *"Everybody thinks I'm this tough guy, and that's not necessarily true. I'm actually really quiet, humble and loyal. I love to make jokes and have a good time. I'm really a people person."*

He also revealed his goal in rapping, *"I don't wanna do nothing else but make good music, stay positive, and be great. And never go broke."*

FBG Duck's turbulent lifestyle and loved ones who died at a young age were frequent topics in his music. In his song, 'OK,' he talks about the reality he had to face as a child having his father locked up. He also spoke about his late brother. Chicago Tribune writes,

"He speaks about having no one to father him and pondered whether things would have been different if his dad had not always been locked up. He talks about "coming away from seeing rats and roaches" to making music for "the folks who feel helpless." He wondered if his older brother, an aspiring rapper, who was shot to death three years ago, would be proud of him for making something of himself. The song seemed to forebode his own death."

"Got a call from 'Lil Bro.' That n**** trying to kill me. Everything gone be OK... If it ever, ever come down to that day. I put some money in the safe just to make sure my kids and my mama 'em straight," he says in the track.

Duck never really made mention of his parents, but in an interview, he said his father had been in jail for 24 years. He grew up at his grandmother's home with his siblings and cousins. He also had a sister named Le Andrea White. Duck has a daughter. In a social media post, he shared a photo of his daughter with the caption,

"My Baby Girl Getting Big On Me Daddy Love You With Every Bone & My Body #DADDYGIRL #MYPRINCESS."

The Chicago Fly Boy Gang

In 2017, the Duck's brother, Jermaine Robinson (FBG Brick), was shot and killed in his Chicago South Side home. He was only 26. During his 2017 interview with VLAD TV, FBG Duck revealed that he had been shot twice. He was also reportedly once stabbed in the stomach by his ex-girlfriend. He revealed that he slapped her before she took a knife and stabbed him. She was arrested, but he pressed no charges.

Though he had been shot twice, he saw no need to leave Chicago as other rappers such as Chief Keef and Lil Durk have done. In an interview, when asked why he didn't move out of Chicago, Duck said he didn't want to leave the people he was familiar with for strangers he didn't trust.

"I got more in Chicago than they got more in Chicago. They're s**t I gotta make sure I take of here first before I do anything. Plus I ain't that type of motherf****r that want to go move to another city because I don't trust nobody. I don't trust new people. I don't want to hang around new people. I don't want no new friends because I don't trust nobody… You can die anywhere. You can get shot anywhere. It's just like in Chicago I know better."

He also explained that the rappers who moved didn't move because they had money but because they were scared.

In 2018, Duck denied rumors that he was shot in the shoulder. He posted a video on his Instagram story stating that he wasn't involved in any shooting. *"Y'All Say Anything On The Internet,"* he wrote in the caption. He later told VLADTV that he didn't like that people on the internet think they know things he's involved in before the truth is even confirmed.

On Tuesday, August 4, 2020, FBG Duck went shopping in the luxury retail plaza within Chicago's upscale Gold Coast neighborhood, just off Michigan Avenue. He stood near a high-end clothing store entrance when two vehicles - a black Ford Taurus and a silver Chrysler 300M pulled up. Four gunmen got out and opened fire, shooting FBG Duck and others before fleeing the scene.

FBG Duck was rushed to Northwestern Hospital. A woman waiting for him in a parked black Mercedes-Benz was injured, as well as a male who was with them. They were both taken to the hospital where the 26-year-old FBG Duck was pronounced dead at 5:06 p.m. He was identified as the deceased victim by police radio traffic and family members on social media.

Duck's relatives said he had gone to the store to purchase a birthday present for his son, one of his four children. Witnesses said an argument broke out, which led to gunfire. Gunshots were reportedly exchanged between two people, and one man ran towards Michigan Avenue. Afterward, additional shots were fired. The glass on a Dolce and Gabbana storefront was shattered during the attack.

Video from the scene was released. It showed Duck and his associates after the shooting, with two men seen lying on the ground in the street with injuries. A woman walks up to the two men and looks with horror, probably shouting. It also shows Duck struggling for his life. The shooting came as a shock because the upscale neighborhood is a place where violence is usually rare.

Deputy Chief for the Chicago Police Department, Daniel O'Shea, said in a statement,

"We don't expect this type of activity in this neighborhood. This area is well policed, and this is something that was specifically targeted for these individuals. To see this happen in the middle of the day is very, very disturbing."

Duck was known to have feuds with other rappers affiliated with rival gangs and released diss tracks insulting several of the opposing gang members. Before his death, Duck released a music video where he made derogatory remarks about slain members of the Black Disciple street gang. Among them was Odee Perry, the murdered gang member from O'Block.

On the day Duck was killed, he reportedly traveled through the city, live-streaming his whereabouts on social media, making it easier for his killers to track him down. In a 2017 interview, Duck said he was aware that a lot of people wanted to kill him, and he was trying to stay out of trouble,

*"Of course I know muthaf****s wanna kill me. I'm a very disrespectful person. I know what I did in my lifetime. They don't know because they don't be out here with me. They don't be on these blocks. You feel me? So they don't know. Can't nobody tell you s**t about me like I could tell you about me. So it's like, why would I put myself in a place where I know I ain't supposed to be? So it's like if I put myself in that place and I know I ain't supposed to be there, then I know I'm looking for trouble."*

He also affirmed that he wasn't going to play with his precious life, *"But I ain't gon' go nowhere I ain't wanted 'cause I ain't gon' play with my life. My life mean a lot."*

In an interview with VladTV, FBG had said that he was too careful and intelligent ever to be gunned down, *"I know what to do and what not to do. How I move around, I'm safe… I'm like a ghost. I can see you, but you can't see me."*

Duck was the third child of his mother to die in a six-year period. In 2014, fire claimed the life of Duck's 3-year-old sister; added to the killing of his brother, Jermaine Robinson, also known as FBG Brick, who was murdered in 2017.

Chicago Tribune stated that Duck's music video was probably the cause of his death,

"Weekly certainly must have known that his latest video would draw the attention of his adversaries and lead to retaliation. One of the characteristics of this genre of music is to project a machismo image that appears to defy death."

Lupe Fiasco, a fellow Chicago rapper, expressed his surprise when he learned of the shooting location,

"On Oak Street?... What type of nonsense? That's right downtown. Wow, dang that's terrible, man. That's terrible. He was really, really good. He's a really good rapper. On Oak Street — that's like somebody getting shot on Rodeo or like on 5th Avenue in New York."

GoodKids MadCity, a student anti-violence group, posted on Twitter.

"RIP @FBG_DUCK we're sending love & light to your family. Our city needs healing."

Chicago community activist Ja'Mal Green said he heard about Duck's death from his friends. He also said his loss would probably lead to retaliation.

"He was pretty popular and, at the end of the day, there are going to be a lot of people angry at this. A lot of young people are going to lose hope because he was an idol. It's going to take the city a large effort to help young people cope with this loss."

Less than a week after her son was killed, FBG Duck's mother, LaSheena Weekly, went to the scene of the shooting to speak against any retaliation for her son's death. *"I am here today to ask for peace in the city of Chicago. I am asking that his fans, friends of my son, to please not seek retaliation in the death of my son...As his mother, I want to say, please put the guns down so that the generation of tomorrow can grow and live a long and healthy life."*

In April 2021, friends and family members of the late Chicago Rapper gathered in the exact spot where he was killed for a memorial. His mother delivered a heartfelt message to the crowd, *"Here in this very spot, where we lost Carlton, also known as FBG Duck, it's been a hard year. It's been a long year. We've accomplished so much within a year of my son's presence not being here. A little bad, mainly good, and my message that I send to y'all from the heart. I really want better for our children, our race, our culture."*

She continued, *"In spite of whatever somebody tried to say, everything you did was for your family, for your friends for your children… and I want to just tell you, your brother and your sister and my momma and everybody whose presence that I feel in me that keep me going because I know what it is. I just want to say thank you God for blessing me with my son for 26 beautiful years."*

Conclusion

The focus of this book has been chiefly on Drill music, especially the city of its origin, Chicago. However, our brief look at the music and the people from around the world revealed how the style of music, crime, and murder are intertwined. It is nearly impossible to separate one from the other. This begs the question, is it the music or the people? Maybe it is even the music and the people.

A critical look at the music itself shows that it is a simple style of music that brings and gives hope to thousands of youth in several hoods across the globe. Young men and women of different races use Drill to tell their stories because it resonates with their abandoned, poverty-stricken communities. This was evident in the Chicago scene where the neighborhood was mostly abandoned and neglected to rot away in crimes and allowed to kill each senselessly.

Some of you who have read this book probably did not believe this was the same glorious United States you have heard about, lived, and come to respect, but it is. If you find the stories in this book unbelievable, you will not be the first. The scenes in Chicago have been likened to war-torn Iraq and Afghanistan. The killing that goes on is so senseless that it is sometimes unimaginable. Often people have wondered what role the authorities played while all of this went on.

For the most part, the role of the police and other stakeholders who should have been in better control of these streets is often confusing. The crimes that have gone down make it seem like the authorities themselves were overwhelmed. There were stories of police involvement in some cases. We are talking about bribery to look the other way, and where this was not the case, it would seem the authorities allowed these gangs to outshoot themselves, then came out later to pick up the pieces.

There are thousands of unsolved cases of young men and women wasted and gone forever that may never be solved. In fairness to the authorities, there have been some serious moves in the past and, most recently, to curb crime and gun violence associated with Drill music; one can only hope that it yields better results than previous efforts.

You have to wonder what role these young parents played in these sad situations. Drill, and violence. How were these kids brought up? We have seen many instances where the parents were either absent or played no role in the lives of these young people. For some, their children only followed in their footsteps to live a life of crime, violence, and street rivalry. Some families have lost their only child in this life of crime. Some families, as we have seen, lost as many as three members to this lifestyle. The Chicago hood is ravaged by families familiar with losses, pains, and depression because they buried their young for many years.

One cannot but feel sorry for the innocent victims and their families. Some had done nothing wrong, other than just going about their everyday business when they were shot, wounded, and killed. Some were even in their houses when the violence came knocking. The lucky ones seem to be those who could get out of Chicago neighborhoods quickly enough before becoming victims.

There is a ray of hope and a sigh of light at the end of the tunnel. Today, from the big names like Lil Durk, and Chief Keef to the upcoming players, everyone for the first time seems to be saying and singing the same lyrics of "enough of the killings." We hope the message will drive home, and everybody will see the need to put the guns away. Education will also play a significant role in reducing the violence and gang lives on the streets. We hope more will be done to keep these young ones engaged and away from the gang and crime lifestyles.

If you have enjoyed this book, do us a favor and leave us a great review on the platform where you purchased it from. We would also appreciate it greatly if you recommend it to your friends and family to read and enjoy.

Update GBG Duck murder

In the recent updates on the O-Block five murder case involving the killing of FBG Duck, six members or associates of the O-Block street gang were found guilty of racketeering offenses, including the murder of FBG Duck, whose real name was Carlton Weekly. The convicted individuals were part of a criminal organization that used violence to protect their gang territories. The jury concluded that they conspired to kill FBG Duck to maintain and improve their positions within the gang.

The six convicted individuals, Charles Liggins, Kenneth Roberson, Tacarlos Offerd, Christopher Thomas, Marcus Smart, and Ralph Turpin, were found guilty of murder in aid of racketeering and are facing mandatory life sentences in federal prison. They will be sentenced in August and September 2024.

These convictions were announced by the authorities, including the Acting U.S. Attorney for the Northern District of Illinois, the FBI, and the Chicago Police Department, with significant support from the Cook County State's Attorney's Office. These developments occurred on January 17, 2024, concerning the trial's outcome and the convictions related to FBG Duck's murder case.

References

Zender, T. (September 8, 2020) A Brief History of Drill Music, Globally. Across the Culture.

https://www.acrosstheculture.com/media/music/history-drill-music/

Oliver- James, C. The Origin of Drill Music and Its Global Impact. Vingt Sept Magazine

https://www.vingtseptmagazine.com/post/the-origins-of-drill-music-and-its-global-impact

Claire, M. (March 24, 2021) Drill Rap Explores Violence and Identity with a Global Audience. The Ford Hamram.

https://thefordhamram.com/80012/culture/drill-rap-explores-violence-and-identity-with-a-global-audience/

Gangster Disciples. The Chicago Gang History (20th Century Gang History)

http://www.chicagoganghistory.com/gang/gangster-disciples/

Black Disciples. The Chicago Gang History (20th Century Gang History)

http://www.chicagoganghistory.com/gang/gangster-disciples/

The FamousPeople.com. Larry Hoover Biography.

https://www.thefamouspeople.com/profiles/larry-hoover-31351.php

Ann, S. T. (December 31, 1996) The Journey of Chicago's Ultimate Street Tough. The Christian Science Monitor.

https://www.csmonitor.com/1996/1231/123196.us.us.1.html

George, W. K. Ph.D. Gang Threat Analysis: The Black Disciples. National Gang Crime Research Center.

https://www.ngcrc.com/ngcrc/bdprofile.html

Nancy, R. G. (September 1994) Murder in Miniature. TIME Magazine.

https://web.archive.org/web/20071117075012/http://www.time.com/time/magazine/article/0,9171,981460-5,00.html

Michael, D. (April 2014) How Chicago Became "Chiraq." Daily Beast

https://www.thedailybeast.com/how-chicago-became-chiraq?ref=scroll

"Hidden America: Don't Shoot, I Want to Grow Up." Statistics Surrounding Gang Violence in Chicago. ABC New.

https://abcnews.go.com/Nightline/fullpage/chicago-gang-violence-numbers-17509042

October 2013. Lil Durk Explains OTF, GBE & 300. Kollege Kidd

https://kollegekidd.com/news/lil-durk-explains-otf-gbe-300/

September 2013. Lil Durk Says He's no Longer GBE. Kollege Kidd

https://kollegekidd.com/news/lil-durk-says-he-is-no-longer-gbe/

Rap Collection from Chicago: Only the Family. Wikipedia

https://en.wikipedia.org/wiki/Only_the_Family

Glory Boys Entertainment. Hip-hop Music Fandom

https://hip-hop-music.fandom.com/wiki/Glory_Boyz_Entertainment

Bert, L. (June 2014). OTF Rap Group. Hipi Wiki

http://www.hipwiki.com/OTF+%28Rap+Group%29

Michael, D. (July 2012). Chicago Rapper Lil Jojo Went to His Grave for Taunting a Rival Gang Member. The Daily Beast.

https://www.thedailybeast.com/chicago-rapper-lil-jojo-went-to-his-grave-for-taunting-a-rival-gang-member?ref=scroll

February 2017. Alleged Gang Member "D. Rose" Gets 40 Years for Teens Murder

https://www.nbcchicago.com/news/local/alleged-gang-member-drose-gets-40-years-for-teens-murder/29922/

Abhir "D. Rose" Sardin Wrongfully Convicted, This is a Petition to Free Him. Charge.org

www.charge.org/sardin

September 2014. D. Rose – 600 Chicago Gang Member. Hipi Wiki

http://www.hipwiki.com/D+Rose-600+Chicago+Gang+Member

Nolan, S. (October 2019). EXCLUSIVE: Chicago Rapper D. Rose Loses Appeal of Murder Conviction

https://allhiphop.com/news/chicago-rapper-d-rose-loses-appeal-of-murder-conviction/

Erica, D. (February 2014). Mom of 14-Year-Old: 'I Never Wanted to be Like the Mothers on TV'. DNA Info Chicago.

https://www.dnainfo.com/chicago/20140213/woodlawn/mom-of-slain-14-year-old-i-never-wanted-be-like-mothers-on-tv/

The Criminal History of RondoNumbaNine. Bridge Race – YouTube.

http://www.hipwiki.com/Cdai

March, 2016. Cdai. Hipi Wiki.

http://www.hipwiki.com/Cdai

Rapper Cdai Charged with Murder in Shooting Death of Livery Javan Boyd Near U.S. Cellular Field. Chicago Homicide Watch.

http://chicago.homicidewatch.org/2014/03/18/courtney-ealy-also-charged-with-murder-in-shooting-death-of-livery-javan-boyd-near-u-s-cellular-field/index.html

Erin, M. & Emily, M. (March 2014). Rapper Cdai Charged in Livery Driver's Murder. DNA Info

https://www.dnainfo.com/chicago/20140318/armour-square/second-person-charged-killing-of-livery-driver.amp/

Interview with Cdai – Only Fans Sent Me Money. VLADTv

https://www.vladtv.com/article/265300/cdai-says-fans-not-600-have-sent-him-money-claims-rondo-turned-on-him

Janine, S. (May 2021). Murder of Chicago Rapper in South Beach 2 Years Ago Identified. Local 10.

https://www.local10.com/news/local/2021/05/20/murderer-of-chicago-rapper-in-south-beach-2-years-ago-identified-miami-beach-detectives-say/

Chicago Rapper AAB Hellabandz Shot and Killed Outside Miami Nightclub.

https://wgntv.com/news/chicago-rapper-aab-hellabandz-shot-and-killed-outside-miami-nightclub/

Sarah, F. Chicago Rapper Identified as Suspect in Fatal 2015 Markham Nightclub Shooting Has Been Killed. Chicago Tribune

https://www.chicagotribune.com/suburbs/daily-southtown/ct-sta-hooper-adriannas-suspect-shot-st-0519-story.html

Lil Durk & His Family Gather After the Death Of OTF DThang

https://www.hotnewhiphop.com/lil-durk-and-his-family-gather-after-the-death-of-otf-dthang-news.133665.html

How did Lil Durk's brother OTF DThang die? What was his cause of death?

https://www.capitalxtra.com/news/lil-durk-brother-otf-dthang-die-cause-of-death-shot-killed-chicago-rapper/

LIL DURK BRAVES A SMILE FOR INSTAGRAM FOLLOWING BROTHER OTF DTHANG'S FUNERAL

https://hiphopdx.com/news/id.62642/title.lil-durk-braves-a-smile-for-instagram-following-brother-otf-dthangs-funeral

RAPPER'S BROTHER Who was rapper Lil Durk's brother OTF DThang?

https://www.the-sun.com/entertainment/3028128/who-rapper-lil-durk-brother-otf-dthang/

Lil Durk's brother, rapper OTF DThang, shot to death outside Harvey strip club

https://wgntv.com/news/chicago-news/lil-durks-brother-rapper-otf-dthang-fatally-shot-outside-harvey-nightclub/

Lil Durk's slain brother's friend sought after cop shot during gunfight at suburban Chicago strip club

https://chicago.suntimes.com/crime/2021/6/15/22535898/lil-durk-rapper-brother-dontay-dthang-banks-dead-murder-club-o-harvey

Lil Durk Shares His First Post Since His Brother DThang's Death

https://www.hotnewhiphop.com/lil-durk-shares-his-first-post-since-his-brother-dthangs-death-news.134362.html

Lil Durk's brother DThang reportedly shot and killed

https://www.revolt.tv/news/2021/6/6/22521280/lil-durks-brother-dthang-reportedly-killed-in-chicago

Lil Durk's Brother, Rapper OTF DThang, Killed

https://www.vibe.com/news/national/lil-durks-brother-dthang-killed-1234620570/amp/

GIRLFRIEND OF LIL DURK'S SLAIN BROTHER DTHANG SPEAKS OUT

https://hiphopdx.com/news/id.62541/title.girlfriend-of-lil-durks-slain-brother-dthang-speaks-out

Lil Durk's Brother OTF DThang Shot and Killed

https://www.xxlmag.com/lil-durk-brother-killed/

Who is Tooka? Chicago gang member and King Von lyrics inspiration

https://www.thefocus.news/music/who-is-tooka/

How Tooka's Death Still Reverberates in Rap Today

https://chaospin.com/how-tookas-death-still-reverberates-in-rap-today/

Mothers of your favorite drill artists

https://youtu.be/cb6XVex0PFk

Mother of Chicago's Tooka Speaks on People Disrespecting Dead Son: 'It Makes Me Upset'

https://www.complex.com/music/2020/12/mother-of-chicago-tooka-speaks-on-people-disrespecting-dead-son

A murdered teen, two million tweets and an experiment to fight gun violence

https://www.nature.com/articles/d41586-018-06169-8

Odee Perry. Perry, Barnes, Rappers - Pinterest

https://www.pinterest.com/amp/pin/783978247617046669/

'O Block': the most dangerous block in Chicago, once home to Michelle Obama

https://www.google.com/amp/s/chicago.suntimes.com/platform/amp/2014/11/2/18458059/o-block-most-dangerous-block-in-chicago-michelle-obama-chief-keef-parkway-gardens-south-king-drive

Man, 20, fatally shot near South Side housing complex

https://www.chicagotribune.com/news/ct-xpm-2011-08-11-chi-man-20-fatally-shot-near-south-side-housing-complex-20110810-story.html

Girl, 17, bragged about 'killing 17 people' online before being gunned down

https://www.mirror.co.uk/news/us-news/girl-17-bragged-killing-17-18927017

Odee Perry. Hip Wiki.

http://www.hipwiki.com/Odee+Perry

US Rapper FBG Duck Killed After Mocking The Death Of Rival Gang Members

https://scenestr.com.au/music/us-rapper-fbg-duck-killed-after-mocking-the-death-of-rival-gang-members-20200806

An Interview with King Von

https://djbooth.net/features/2020-12-21-king-von-interview-audiomack

The day O block was made

https://youtu.be/F6ePhdjfQIU

The reason Odee Perry got caught lacking

https://youtu.be/lFE5aFpEwmE

Gakirah Barnes: The 17-year old Assassin

https://youtu.be/gZUM4YbCS88

Odee Perry - The Chiraq story "Legend of O'Block" Reaction Chiraq Street Legends Chiraq Drill https://youtu.be/SNXAEFZ9EAE

King Von Killed Notorious Teenage Gangster Gakirah Barnes Says Police Report

https://urbanislandz.com/2021/07/13/king-von-killed-notorious-teenage-gangster-gakirah-barnes-says-police-report/

A murdered teen, two million tweets and an experiment to fight gun violence

https://www.nature.com/articles/d41586-018-06169-8

GANGSTER GIRL How promising student was drawn into gangland world and went on to viciously 'kill 17' and brag about crimes online – before being murdered at 17

https://www.thesun.co.uk/news/9686479/teen-girl-gangster-gakirah-barnes/

4 dead among at least 36 shot in Chicago in 36 hours

https://www.chicagotribune.com/news/ct-xpm-2014-04-13-chi-chicago-shootings-at-least-4-dead-among-35-shot-20140413-story.html

'She called herself a hitta' — a 17-year-old female assassin operated on the South Side

https://chicago.suntimes.com/2015/7/23/18588969/garkirah-barnes-teenage-female-assassin-gangster-disciples-chicago-gang-hitta

Teen found dead in South Side alley

https://www.chicagotribune.com/news/breaking/chi-man-found-dead-in-south-side-alley-20111111-story.html

Rodney Boss Trell Stewart

http://www.hipwiki.com/Rodney+Boss+Trell+Stewart

KING VON NAMED IN 2014 FATAL SHOOTING OF GAKIRAH BARNES

https://thesource.com/2021/07/13/king-von-named-in-2014-fatal-shooting-of-gakirah-barnes/

Gakirah K.I Barnes Final hours

https://youtu.be/nSso8gOEb0Q

The story of female Assassin Gakirah KI Barnes

https://youtu.be/oV_9xy_UAvM

Chicago Gangster Ep 9 - Gakirah Barnes (KI)

https://youtu.be/OsiP1hCC4Hw

Chicago American Gangster, Gakirah Barnes aka K.I from Tookaville/STL

https://youtu.be/EUpowy0Q5ck

CSL reloaded Ep 1: From Gakirah Barnes to K I

https://youtu.be/X8VoxhFe3Ss

Lil Reese, rapper involved in Chief Keef and JoJo feud, tied to video beating

https://web.archive.org/web/20121027012558/http://www.suntimes.com/news/metro/15966048-418/lil-reese-rapper-involved-in-chief-keef-and-jojo-feud-tied-to-video-beating.html

South Side rapper Lil Reese is found sleeping in car and arrested on warrant https://web.archive.org/web/20130503174419/http://articles.chicagotribune.com/2013-04-29/news/ct-met-chicago-rapper-warrant-0429-20130429_1_arrest-warrant-chief-keef-lil-reese

Lil Reese Found Sleeping in Car, Arrested On A Warrant

https://web.archive.org/web/20130702210342/http://www.hiphopdx.com/index/news/id.23740/title.lil-reese-found-sleeping-in-car-arrested-on-a-warrant/

LIL REESE ARRESTED, CHARGED WITH AUTO THEFT

https://hiphopdx.com/news/id.24431/title.lil-reese-arrested-charged-with-auto-theft#

Lil Reese Arrested for Drug Possession

https://web.archive.org/web/20150524193223/http://www.hiphopdx.com/index/news/id.24676/title.lil-reese-arrested-for-drug-possession

RAPPER LIL REESE GRAZED IN EYE DURING SHOOTING ...Pics of Bloody Aftermath

https://www.tmz.com/2021/05/15/rapper-lil-reese-shot-again-chicago/

RAPPER LIL REESE SHOT IN THE NECK, IN CRITICAL CONDITION. Cops Investigating In Illinois

https://www.tmz.com/2019/11/11/rapper-lil-reese-shot-neck-chicago-illinois-critical-condition/

Chicago rapper Lil Reese critically wounded in shooting at Country Club Hills intersection

https://wgntv.com/news/police-respond-to-reports-of-shooting-in-country-club-hills/

Lil Reese Says He Had 'Hella Luck' Discharge from Hospital Following Shooting

https://www.billboard.com/articles/columns/hip-hop/8543926/lil-reese-gives-update-shooting

Lil Reese Sends Racist Tweet About Coronavirus

https://www.hotnewhiphop.com/lil-reese-sends-racist-tweet-about-coronavirus-news.106107.html

Lil Reese Twitter Suspended Over Racist Coronavirus Tweet

https://urbanislandz.com/2020/03/16/lil-reese-twitter-suspended-over-racist-coronavirus-tweet/

Lil Reese

https://en.wikipedia.org/wiki/Lil_Reese#cite_note-15

Lil Reese breaks silence after being shot in Chicago

https://www.revolt.tv/news/2021/5/21/22448138/lil-reese-breaks-silence-shot

New details still leave questions about shootout that wounded rapper Lil Reese in a Near North parking garage

https://chicago.suntimes.com/crime/2021/5/17/22440481/lil-reese-shooting-north-side-parking-garage-grand

Lil Reese says he wants $1 Million for his first post-shooting interview

https://www.thefader.com/2019/11/17/lil-reese-wants-1-million-interview

Lil Reese Has Been Arrested on Indirect Criminal Contempt Charges https://www.complex.com/music/2016/01/lil-reese-arrested-on-indirect-criminal-contempt-charges?utm_campaign=musictw&utm_source=twitter&utm_medium=social

Rapper Lil Reese, 2 others shot on Near North Side in apparent gunfight over stolen car, authorities say

https://www.chicagotribune.com/news/breaking/ct-chicago-shooting-near-north-side-20210515-

phkabdszxjeu7mhi3lsyn4exq4-story.html

Lil Reese: Family, Net Worth , Parents, Wife , Children, Real Name and Biography

https://haqexpress.com/Lil-Reese

Lil Reese: 5 Things to Know About the Chicago Rapper, 28, Reportedly Shot Again

https://hollywoodlife.com/feature/who-is-lil-reese-rapper-3790872/

Lil Reese Speaks on Chicago Shooting, Refutes Domestic Violence Claims

https://www.vibe.com/music/music-news/lil-reese-interview-shooting-domestic-violence-claims-1234621599/

Lil Reese Denies Hitting His Girlfriend After Arrest Over Domestic Violence

https://urbanislandz.com/2021/06/05/lil-reese-denies-hitting-his-girlfriend-after-arrest-over-domestic-violence/

Fredo Santana dies: Rapper who appeared in Drake video passes away age 27 https://www.independent.co.uk/arts-entertainment/music/news/fredo-santana-dead-rapper-drake-video-27-friend-maxo-kream-instagram-a8169521.html

Chicago Rapper Fredo Santana Dies at 27

https://www.billboard.com/articles/columns/hip-hop/8095243/chicago-rapper-fredo-santana-dies-at-27

Fredo Santana

https://en.wikipedia.org/wiki/Fredo_Santana

Fredo Santana Taken to Hospital After Having a Seizure

https://www.xxlmag.com/fredo-santana-hospital-seizure/

Fredo Santana's Cause of Death Includes Cardiovascular Disease and Epilepsy

https://www.xxlmag.com/fredo-santanas-cause-of-death-cardiovascular-disease-and-epilepsy/

RUSS CAUSES CONTROVERSY WITH ANTI-DRUG SHIRT

https://www.xxlmag.com/russ-made-10-million-dollars-from-independent-catalog/

Watch a posthumously released music video for Fredo Santana's "Some Money"

https://www.thefader.com/2019/09/19/watch-a-posthumously-released-music-video-for-fredo-santanas-some-money

CHIEF KEEF WANTS SMOKE WITH ANYONE WHO SAYS LEAN KILLED FREDO SANTANA

https://thesource.com/2020/03/05/chief-keef-wants-smoke-with-anyone-who-says-lean-killed-fredo-santana/

Cause of death determined for Chicago rapper Fredo Santana

https://www.chicagotribune.com/entertainment/music/ct-ent-fredo-santana-cause-of-death-determined-20180808-story.html

Chicago rapper Fredo Santana dead at age 27

https://www.chicagotribune.com/entertainment/music/ct-ent-fredo-santana-dead-20180120-story.html

Chicago Rapper Fredo Santana Dead at 27

https://www.rollingstone.com/music/music-news/chicago-rapper-fredo-santana-dead-at-27-123554/

Lil Durk's manager shot dead in Chicago

https://www.pulse.ng/entertainment/celebrities/uchenna-agina-lil-durks-manager-shot-dead-in-chicago/l9tryc4

Rapper Lil Durk's Manager Killed in Chicago

https://www.billboard.com/articles/news/6516815/rapper-lil-durk-manager-uchenna-agina-killed-in-chicago

Rapper Lil Durk's Manager Fatally Shot Hours After Meeting With Joakim Noah

https://www.dnainfo.com/chicago/20150327/avalon-park/man-fatally-shot-avalon-park-police-say

How Nigerian Artiste Manager, Uchenna Agina, Was Killed In America

https://www.thenigerianvoice.com/movie/174450/how-nigerian-artiste-manager-uchenna-agina-was-killed-in-a.html

Joakim Noah vows to stay active

https://www.espn.com/chicago/nba/story/_/id/12579801/joakim-noah-chicago-bulls-mourns-loss-uchenna-agina

Bulls' Joakim Noah discusses murder of Lil Durk manager 'Chino Dolla'

http://chicago.homicidewatch.org/2015/03/28/bulls-joakim-noah-discusses-murder-of-lil-durk-manager-chino-dolla/index.html

Lil' Durk's Manager Chino Dolla Shot And Killed In Chicago

https://allhiphop.com/news/lil-durks-manager-chino-dolla-shot-and-killed-in-chicago/

Lil Durk's Manager OTF Chino Shot and Killed in Chicago

https://www.vice.com/en/article/rnwbaz/lil-durks-manager-otf-chino-shot-and-killed-in-chicago

LIL DURK'S MANAGER SHOT AND KILLED

https://www.xxlmag.com/lil-durks-manager-killed-chicago/

Slain manager of Chicago rapper had just met with Bulls' star about anti-violence group

https://www.chicagotribune.com/news/breaking/chi-manager-of-chicago-rapper-lil-durk-slain-on-south-side-20150327-story.html

Lil Durk's Manager Uchenna Agina Killed Hours After Meeting with Chicago Bulls' Joachim Noah for Anti-

Violence Campaign

https://www.musictimes.com/articles/33447/20150327/lil-durks-manager-uchenna-agina-killed-hours-meeting-chicago-bulls.htm

Lil Durk's Manager Was Shot and Killed in Chicago Last Night https://www.complex.com/music/2015/03/lil-durk-manager-shot-and-killed

Def Jam rapper's manager killed in a car park after planning anti-violence initiatives

https://www.nme.com/news/music/various-artists-1217-1208537

Lil Durk on OTF Chino Getting Killed (Flashback)

https://youtu.be/2MXyMkIEqvk

Lil Durk's Manager OTF Chino Reportedly Shot Dead in Chicago

https://hiphop24x7.com/news/lil-durks-manager-otf-chino-reportedly-shot-dead-in-chicago/

Chicago rapper FBG Duck killed in brazen daytime shopping attack

https://www.bbc.com/news/world-us-canada-53670653

FBG DUCK: 4 THINGS TO KNOW ABOUT RAPPER GUNNED DOWN IN TRIPLE SHOOTING

https://guardian.ng/life/fbg-duck-4-things-to-know-about-rapper-gunned-down-in-triple-shooting/

Memorial held for FBG Duck in Chicago one year after his death

https://www.revolt.tv/news/2021/8/8/22616032/fbg-duck-anniversary-memorial

Chicago rapper FBG Duck, 26, is Shot Dead in Broad-Daylight Drive-by in Neighborhood Lined with Designer Boutiques as Violence Surges in the Windy City Where Murders are Up 152 Percent

https://www.dailymail.co.uk/news/article-8594151/Chicago-rapper-FBG-Duck-26-shot-dead-brazen-broad-daylight-drive-by.html

FBG Duck, Chicago Rapper, Dead at 26

https://pitchfork.com/news/fbg-duck-chicago-rapper-dead-at-26/

Column: FBG Duck brought a street fight between the 'have-nots' into the turf controlled by the 'haves'

https://www.chicagotribune.com/columns/dahleen-glanton/ct-fbg-duck-gold-coast-shooting-20200810-w25ka6xgbjdipik7m2twcqgmmu-story.html

RESURFACED FBG DUCK INTERVIEW REVEALS HE KNEW HIS LIFE WAS MARKED

https://hiphopdx.com/news/id.57209/title.resurfaced-fbg-duck-interview-reveals-he-knew-his-life-was-marked#

Rapper FBG Duck shot to death in brazen Chicago ambush

https://www.ajc.com/news/rapper-fbg-duck-shot-to-death-in-brazen-chicago-ambush/GRVRVHNI5ZA43AZ34GMYN3BTCU/

FBG DUCK SHOT AND KILLED IN CHICAGO

https://www.xxlmag.com/fbg-duck-shot/

FBG Duck Death, Age, Height, Family, Net worth & Biography

https://www.celebsweek.com/fbg-duck/

FBG Duck (Rapper): Real Name, Biography, Family, Marriage, Career, Death and Net Worth!

https://besttoppers.com/fbg-duck/

FBG Duck

https://biographymask.com/fbg-duck/

FBG Duck's Brother Was Killed in a Shooting Just Three Years Ago

https://visionviral.com/fbg-ducks-brother-was-killed-in-a-shooting-just-three-years-ago/

FBG Duck on Getting Shot Twice, Ex-Girlfriend Stabbing Him

https://youtu.be/HpuhDV-gfnc

Prosecutors: Man arrested at rapper's house pulled trigger in 2009 killing

https://www.chicagotribune.com/news/breaking/chi-bail-denied-for-alleged-triggerman-in-2009-fatal-shooting-20141107-story.html

Lil Durk Calls for OTF Affiliate Baybay's Freedom Amid Murder Charge

https://kollegekidd.com/news/lil-durk-calls-for-otf-affiliate-baybay-freedom-amid-murder-charge/

THF Zoo

https://sglyric.com/artists/1488338/thf-zoo

The Criminal History of THF Zoo

https://www.youtube.com/watch?v=1YOYfJ7_M-k

Lil Durk and King Von Atlanta incident

https://weaponsg.com/lil-durk-king-von-case/

Bayzoo

https://chiraqwikifacts.fandom.com/wiki/Bayzoo

#bayzoo Instagram posts

https://www.picuki.com/tag/bayzoo

051 Melly

http://www.hipwiki.com/051+Melly

051 Melly Shot Dead: Chicago's Yarmel Williams killed in shooting at party

https://www.monstersandcritics.com/music/051-melly-shot-dead-chicagos-yarmel-williams-killed-in-shooting-at-party/

King Louie Affiliate, Mubu Krump, Shot and Killed in South Side Chicago

https://kollegekidd.com/news/king-louie-affiliate-mubu-krump-shot-and-killed-in-south-side-chicago/

No bail for man charged in May slaying of 15-year-old boy in Bronze Ville

https://www.chicagotribune.com/news/breaking/ct-man-charged-in-may-slaying-of-boy-15-in-bronzeville-20150614-story.html

Chicago Rapper "Blood Money" Slain in West Englewood

https://chicago.cbslocal.com/2014/04/10/chicago-rapper-blood-money-slain-in-west-englewood/

Blood money

https://hip-hop-music.fandom.com/wiki/Blood_Money

Chicago Rapper Big Glo, Chief Keef's Cousin, Shot Dead at 33

https://www.thefader.com/2014/04/10/chicago-rapper-big-glo-chief-keefs-cousin-shot-dead-at-33

Big Glo Dead: Slain Rapper Was Chief Keef's Cousin

https://www.dnainfo.com/chicago/20140410/west-englewood/big-glo-dead-slain-rapper-was-chief-keefs-cousin

Chief Keef's cousin Big Glo shot to death in Englewood

https://www.chicagotribune.com/news/breaking/chi-blood-money-big-glo-chief-keef-englewood-chicago-20140410-story.html

Family Says Blood Money Was Murdered Out of Jealousy After Inking Interscope Deal

https://kollegekidd.com/news/family-says-blood-money-was-murdered-out-of-jealousy-after-inking-interscope-deal/

Chief Keef's Glo Gang Artist, Blood Money, Murdered in Shooting

https://kollegekidd.com/news/chief-keef-glo-gang-blood-money-dead/

Rapper Big Glo shot dead in West Englewood

https://homicide615.rssing.com/chan-67377865/latest.php

Cousin of Rapper Chief Keef Shot to Death

https://www.nbcchicago.com/news/national-international/chicago-shooting-5600-south-elizabeth-street/72773/

Slain rapper Big Glo laid to rest; father vows better life for children

http://chicago.homicidewatch.org/2014/04/18/slain-rapper-big-glo-laid-to-rest-father-vows-better-life-for-children/index.html

PHOTO GALLERY: Memorial for slain rapper Big Glo

http://chicago.homicidewatch.org/2014/04/10/photo-gallery-memorial-for-slain-rapper-blood-money/index.html

Rapper Big Glo shot dead in West Englewood

http://chicago.homicidewatch.org/2014/04/10/rapper-blood-money-shot-dead-in-west-englewood/index.html

Big Glo's Last Interview: Rough Chicago Upbringing

https://www.youtube.com/watch?v=pW8I54VJ6GY

Big Glo's Last Interview: I'm Chief Keef's Enforcer

https://www.youtube.com/watch?v=DunBR3kzif8

Chicago Rapper Big Glo Shot to Death at Age 33

https://www.spin.com/2014/04/big-glo-shot-to-death-blood-money-chief-keef/

Today in Hip-Hop: R.I.P. Big Glo (February 13, 1984 – April 9, 2014)

https://www.xxlmag.com/today-in-hip-hop-r-i-p-big-glo-february-13-1984-april-9-2014/

Big Glo -- Chief Keef's cousin -- shot to death in Englewood

https://www.sun-sentinel.com/redeye-chief-keefs-rapper-cousin-big-glo-shot-to-death-20140410-story.html

Chief Keef Previews 'Bang 3,' Says Big Glo's Death 'Told Me 'You Gotta Grow Up''

https://www.billboard.com/articles/columns/the-juice/6627348/chief-keef-bang-3-big-glo-death-grow-up

Big Glo

https://www.famousbirthdays.com/people/big-glo.html

CHIEF KEEF'S COUSIN BIG GLO A.K.A. BLOOD MONEY MURDERED IN CHICAGO, ILLINOIS

https://hiphopdx.com/news/id.28248/title.chief-keefs-cousin-big-glo-a-k-a-blood-money-murdered-in-chicago-illinois#

Chief Keef's Cousin Big Glo Gunned Down In Chicago

https://www.ballerstatus.com/2014/04/10/chief-keefs-cousin-big-glo-gunned-chicago/

Chief Keef Reveals Blood Money aka Big Glo Was A Gangster Disciple

https://kollegekidd.com/news/chief-keef-reveals-blood-money-aka-big-glo-was-a-gangster-disciple/

OTF Nunu Dead: Rapper, Cousin of Lil Durk, Fatally Shot

https://www.dnainfo.com/chicago/20140601/englewood/otf-nunu-cousin-of-lil-durk-fatally-shot

OTF Nunu

https://rap.fandom.com/wiki/OTF_Nunu

OTF Nunu, Chicago rapper, shot to death in Chatham

https://abc7chicago.com/otf-nunu-mcarthur-swindle-death-dead/89266/

TEKASHI 6IX9INE 'MOURNS' LIL DURK'S MURDERED COUSIN OTF NUNU IN LATEST CHICAGO TROLLING

https://hiphopdx.com/news/id.57572/title.tekashi-6ix9ine-mourns-lil-durks-murdered-cousin-otf-nunu-in-latest-chicago-trolling

Today in Hip-Hop: R.I.P. OTF NuNu (October 15, 1992 – May 31, 2014)

https://www.xxlmag.com/today-in-hip-hop-r-i-p-otf-nunu-october-15-1992-may-31-2014/

Lil Durk's cousin, rapper OTF Nunu, murdered in Chicago

https://chicagodefender.com/lil-durks-cousin-rapper-otf-nunu-murdered-in-chicago/

RondoNumbaNine Pays Respects to OTF NuNu From Jail

https://kollegekidd.com/news/rondonumbanine-pays-respects-to-otf-nunu-from-jail/

Chicago Rapper OTF Nunu Reportedly Shot and Killed in a Parking Lot

https://www.complex.com/music/2014/05/otf-nunu-shot-killed-lil-durk-affiliate-chicago-parking-lot

OTF Nunu: Chicago Rapper, 21, Shot &Killed In Parking Lot

https://hollywoodlife.com/2014/06/02/otfu-nunu-shot-killed-nuski-rapper-dead/

Lil Durk Shares Rare Photo Of Himself and OTF Nunu

https://kollegekidd.com/news/lil-durk-shares-rare-photo-of-himself-and-otf-nunu/

CHICAGO RAPPER LIL MARC DEAD AFTER SHOOTING

https://www.mtv.com/news/1725143/chicago-rapper-lil-marc-dead-after-shooting/

LIL DURK AND OTF NUNU COLLABORATE ON "OC"

https://thesource.com/2014/04/14/lil-durk-and-otf-nunu-collaborate-on-oc/

King Von - Wikipedia

https://en.m.wikipedia.org/wiki/King_Von

King Von, Emerging Chicago Rapper, Dead At 26

https://www.npr.org/2020/11/06/932178314/king-von-emerging-chicago-rapper-dead-at-26

Rapper King Von Killed in Atlanta Shooting

https://www.vulture.com/2020/11/rapper-king-von-killed-atlanta-shooting-details.html

Savannah man charged with murder in Chicago rapper King Von's death released on $100,000 bond

https://www.savannahnow.com/story/news/2021/03/29/savannah-man-charged-murder-chicago-rapper-king-von-released-bond-jail-free-lul-lil-tim-quando-rondo/7050322002/

King Von: Latest News, Songs, Interviews and Albums

https://www.complex.com/tag/king-von

King Von's ex-manager reveals the late rapper has about 300 unreleased songs

https://www.revolt.tv/news/2021/2/26/22303873/king-von-manager-300-unreleased-songs

Rapper King Von's killing puts a spotlight on Chicago gang ties to Atlanta

https://chicago.suntimes.com/2020/11/13/21561328/king-von-atlanta-chicago-gang-ties-black-disciples-oblock-o-block

King Von's Christmas cash giveaway showed his 'humanity,' anti-violence activist recallshttps://chicago.suntimes.com/2020/11/11/21560956/king-von-mask-tamar-manasseh-david-barksdale-drill-black-gangster-disciples-chicago

Lil Durk Honors King Von with New Memory Tag Chain

https://www.complex.com/style/lil-durk-honors-king-von-new-memory-tag-chain

JEWELER CLEARS THE AIR ON CONTROVERSIAL KING VON CHAIN "I HAVE NOTHING BUT LOVE FOR LIL DURK"

https://thesource.com/2021/01/17/jeweler-clears-the-air-on-controversial-king-von-chain-i-have-nothing-but-love-for-lil-durk/

King Von Gets Posthumous New Video for "Demon"

https://www.google.com/amp/s/pitchfork.com/news/king-von-gets-posthumous-new-video-for-demon-watch/amp/

Dead rapper King Von named as killer of 17-year-old girl who murdered a dozen people

https://www.mirror.co.uk/3am/celebrity-news/dead-rapper-king-von-named-24544564

Lil Durk breaks silence about King Von's death

https://www.revolt.tv/platform/amp/news/2020/11/6/21553510/lil-durk-breaks-silence-king-vons-death

King Von, Up-and-Coming Chicago Rapper, Shot and Killed in Atlanta

https://www.nytimes.com/2020/11/06/arts/music/king-von-dead.html

Quando Rondo Addresses King Von's Fatal Shooting in "End of Story" https://www.complex.com/music/2020/11/quando-rondo-king-von-end-of-story-song

The truth about King Von's parents and his kids

https://thenetline.com/the-truth-about-king-von-parents-and-his-kids/

6ix9ine brutally disrespects king con after Lil Durk visits O'Block mural

https://www.hotnewhiphop.com/6ix9ine-brutally-disrespects-king-von-after-lil-durk-visits-o-block-mural-news.137185.html

WHAT HAPPENED WITH TEKASHI 6IX9INE AND KING VON? RAPPER SENDS ANOTHER DISS

https://www.hitc.com/en-gb/2021/03/04/tekashi-6ix9ine-king-von/?amp

King Von's Manager Responds to Asian Doll Saying She Knew Late Rapper's Last Words

https://www.complex.com/music/2020/11/king-von-manager-responds-asian-doll-late-rapper-last-words

An Interview with King Von

https://djbooth.net/features/2020-12-21-king-von-interview-audiomack

Hip hop pays respects to King Von following his untimely death

https://www.revolt.tv/news/2020/11/6/21552950/hip-hop-king-von-death

KING VON'S SISTER, KAYLA B., CONFIRMS HE HAS ANOTHER CHILD ON THE WAY

https://bckonline.com/2021/06/14/king-vons-sister-kayla-b-confirms-he-has-another-child-on-the-way/amp/

Chief Keef

https://en.wikipedia.org/wiki/Chief_Keef

Chief Keef Charged with Driving 110 MPH In A 55 MPH Zone

https://www.xxlmag.com/chief-keef-charged-with-driving-110-mph-in-a-55-mph-zone/

Chief Keef is going back to jail

https://www.xxlmag.com/chief-keef-going-back-jail/

New Lawsuit Claims Chief Keef Hates Cancer Charities

https://theurbandaily.com/2843981/chief-keef-cancer-charity-lawsuit/

Rapper Chief Keef Arrested for 'Violent Home Invasion' of Producer (Photos) - https://www.thewrap.com/chief-keef-arrested-violent-home-invasion-producer-ramsay-tha-great/

Chief Keef arrested for DUI

https://www.xxlmag.com/chief-keef-arrested-dui/

Chief Keef pleads no contest to possessing controlled substance - https://www.argusleader.com/story/news/crime/2019/04/26/rapper-chief-keef-keith-cozart-marijuana-charge-south-dakota/3579089002/

Back from the dead 2/Big Gucci Sosa - https://pitchfork.com/reviews/albums/20027-chief-keef-gucci-mane-back-from-the-dead-2big-gucci-sosa/

Chief Keef, Lupe Fiasco Feud Is Deeper Than Rap, No I.D. Says - http://www.mtv.com/news/1693628/chief-keef-lupe-fiasco-feud-no-id/

Chief Keef Disses Lupe Fiasco on Twitter, Lupe Responds - https://www.complex.com/music/2012/09/chief-keef-disses-lupe-fiasco-on-twitter-lupe-responds

Lupe Fiasco Squashes Chief Keef Beef

https://www.fuse.tv/2012/09/lupe-fiasco-squashes-chief-keef-beef

Common Says He Respects Chief Keef For Being Raw & Real In His Music - https://hiphopdx.com/news/id.31529/title.common-says-he-respects-chief-keef-for-being-raw-real-in-his-music#

Rhymefest Blasts Chief Keef, Interscope Over Promoting Violent Music - https://hiphopdx.com/news/id.20246/title.rhymefest-blasts-chief-keef-interscope-over-promoting-violent-music

Rap's Killer New Rhymes

https://www.salon.com/2012/12/18/raps_killer_new_rhymes/

6ix9ine Flies Chief Keef's Rumored Baby's Mother to NYC for Gucci Shopping Spree
https://www.xxlmag.com/6ix9ine-chief-keef-baby-mama-shopping-spree/

Tekashi 6ix9ine Admits to Offering $20,000 To Shoot at Chief Keef -https://thesource.com/2019/02/12/tekashi-6ix9ine-admits-to-offering-20000-to-shoot-at-chief-keef/

Chief Keef reveals he's in the hospital

https://www.revolt.tv/news/2021/2/2/22263239/chief-keef-hospitalized

Chief Keef Biography

https://www.hiphopscriptures.com/chief-keef

Chief Keef Is an Icon in an Industry He Doesn't Care For - https://www.complex.com/music/2020/08/chief-keef-industry-doesnt-care-for-25-birthday

Chief Keef

https://pitchfork.com/artists/30357-chief-keef/

Chief Keef Returns with Brand New Song and Video For "The Talk - https://www.ballerstatus.com/2021/07/14/chief-keef-returns-with-brand-new-song-and-video-for-the-talk/

Chief Keef

https://familytron.com/chief-keef/

Tray Savage, Chief Keef Associate, Dead at 26

https://www.complex.com/music/2020/06/tray-savage-dead-at-26

Chief Keef Glo Gang Rapper YNC Capo Killed During Alleged Carjacking - https://hiphopdx.com/news/id.64000/title.chief-keef-glo-gang-rapper-ync-capo-killed-during-carjacking

Chicago rapper Fredo Santana, cousin of Chief Keef, dies at 27 - https://chicago.suntimes.com/2018/1/21/18377985/chicago-rapper-fredo-santana-cousin-of-chief-keef-dies-at-27

Man charged with killing Chicago rapper Tray Savage after identified in video of shooting - https://chicago.suntimes.com/crime/2021/4/26/22403837/tray-savage-murder-charge-demitri-jackson-chief-keef

Chief Keef Asked If He's A Blood, Confirms Gang Affiliation

https://kollegekidd.com/news/chief-keef-asked-if-hes-a-blood-confirms-gang-affiliation/

Chief Keef

http://www.hipwiki.com/Chief+Keef

Chief Keef vs. Chicago: Why the Rapper Has Become Public Enemy No. 1 - https://www.billboard.com/articles/news/6649099/chief-keef-chicago-concert-shut-down-rahm-emanuel-mayor-hologram

LIL JOJO SHOT AND KILLED—TODAY IN HIP-HOP

https://www.xxlmag.com/today-in-hip-hop-r-i-p-lil-jojo/

Lupe Fiasco: Chief Keef Scares me

https://www.bet.com/news/music/2012/08/30/lupe-fiasco-chief-keef-scares-me.html

Takeshi 6ix9ine hospitalized after mixing Weight loss pills and McDonalds coffee - https://www.billboard.com/articles/columns/hip-hop/9459075/tekashi-6ix9ine-hospitalized/

Tekashi 6ix9ine Sentenced To 2 Years in Racketeering Case - https://m.guardian.ng/life/tekashi-6ix9ine-sentenced-to-2-years-in-racketeering-case/

Tekashi 6ix9ine 'Planning Two New Albums' During House Arrest - https://m.guardian.ng/life/tekashi-6ix9ine-planning-two-new-albums-during-house-arrest/

Hologram Performance by Chief Keef Is Shut Down by Police - https://www.nytimes.com/2015/07/27/arts/music/hologram-performance-by-chief-keef-is-shut-down-by-police.html

The End.

www.ingramcontent.com/pod-product-compliance
Lightning Source LLC
Chambersburg PA
CBHW050106170426
43198CB00014B/2479